# NEBS
# MANAGEMENT
# DEVELOPMENT

**SUPER** S E R I E S

## THIRD EDITION

**Managing Information**

# Writing
# Effectively

Published for _____

**&NEBS** Management *by*

Pergamon
*Flexible*
Learning

OXFORD  AMSTERDAM  BOSTON  LONDON  NEW YORK  PARIS
SAN DIEGO  SAN FRANCISCO  SINGAPORE  SYDNEY  TOKYO

Pergamon Flexible Learning
An imprint of Elsevier Science
Linacre House, Jordan Hill, Oxford OX2 8DP
225 Wildwood Avenue, Woburn, MA 01801-2041

First published 1986
Second edition 1991
Third edition 1997
Reprinted 1998, 1999, 2000, 2002

**British Library Cataloguing in Publication Data**
A catalogue record for this book is available from the British Library

ISBN 0 7506 3331 X

The views expressed in this work are those
of the authors and do not necessarily reflect
those of the National Examining Board for
Supervision and Management or of the publisher.

NEBS Management Project Manager: Diana Thomas
Author: Howard Senter
Editor: Grace Belfiore
Series Editor: Diana Thomas
Based on previous material by: Howard Senter & Diana Thomas
Composition by Genesis Typesetting, Rochester, Kent
Printed and bound in Great Britain

# Contents

# Workbook introduction

## 1  NEBS Management Super Series 3 study links

Here are the workbook titles in each module which link with *Writing Effectively*, should you wish to extend your study to other Super Series workbooks. There is a brief description of each workbook in the User Guide.

## 2 S/NVQ links

This workbook relates to the following elements:

A1.3 Make recommendations for improvements to work activities
D1.1 Gather required information
D1.2 Inform and advise others

It will also help you develop the following Personal Competence:

- communicating.

## 3 Workbook objectives

Communicating is what management is all about. You have to lead, motivate, instruct, advise and persuade your team, your own managers and your customers, and you do it by communicating. Research actually shows that communication takes up more than half of most managers' time.

Most of that communication consists of talking and listening to others. Writing plays a smaller, but highly significant part:

- it reaches more people;
- it goes on the record;
- it can travel through time and space;
- wherever it goes it carries an impression of you, your skills and your personality.

If you want to get on in life, your speaking skills will be extremely important, but so will your writing skills.

These are both skills that all managers, supervisors and team leaders need to develop.

- Take Stefan. He was famous for his blunt speaking and ability to 'get things done' but when he moved into a management role, and had to do more of his communicating in writing, he was embarrassed. His spelling wasn't very good, and he somehow couldn't discover how to put things clearly without sounding aggressive.

- Or take Rosie. She had spent a couple of years working in a solicitor's office, and never used a short word when a longer one was available. Her notes and memos became famous for agonizing circumlocutions, which some people in her company found very funny.

Both Stefan and Rosie suffered from their lack of skill in writing in that:

■ they found it harder to get their messages through;
■ their personal credibility was at risk.

Written communication skill is not about learning to be a poet or a novelist. It is about becoming a more effective person. A person who can get through to other people, make them understand, and get results. A person who grows in stature by becoming a better communicator.

In this workbook we will think about where and why writing tends to work better than speech, and vice versa. We will explain how to make sure that written communications reach their target and get the reader's attention; just as importantly, we'll help you improve the impression your written material gives to the reader. As part of this, we'll consider how you can help your readers by keeping your writing short and simple, and using simple tables and graphics. Last but not least, we will think about making notes and filling in forms.

# 3.1 Objectives

On completion of this workbook you will be better able to:

■ decide when it is more useful to write than to speak, and when a combination of the two is even more useful;

■ give your written communications a better chance of:

　■ reaching their destination
　■ being noticed
　■ being read
　■ being understood;

■ remind yourself of ideas, messages and events by making clear and legible notes.

## 4 Activity planner

The following Activities require some planning so you may want to look at these now.

- In Activity 11 you are asked to analyse the kind of written documents that you produce.
- Activity 24 asks you to start compiling your own 'writer's handbook'.
- Activity 36 suggests that you collect and comment on situations where it would be useful to make notes.
- Activity 38 asks you to practise your note-taking skills. You will need to identify a suitable opportunity to do this.

**Portfolio of evidence**

Some or all of these Activities may provide the basis of evidence for your S/NVQ portfolio. All portfolio activities and the Work-based assignment are sign posted with this icon.

The icon states the elements to which the portfolio activities and Work-based assignment relate.

# Session A Why and when to write

## 1 Introduction

We communicate because we need to. The whole of our social and economic structures depend on it. Our spoken languages are very powerful and flexible: before people invented writing, speech was the only way to pass wisdom, history, stories, skills and ideas on from one generation to the next. Human societies managed with speech alone for hundreds of thousands of years.

Spoken language has its limits, however. As soon as humans got involved in large-scale activities, including business, they found they needed something more.

Suppose you have made a contract with a stock breeder to buy 20 pigs in six months time, providing 100 lengths of timber in payment. How do you record the details that you have agreed? If there was only one such contract, you would probably state the terms in front of witnesses, so that everyone concerned would remember them. The room for disputes about what precisely was agreed would be small.

But no-one would trust human memory to recall the exact details of 20, or 100, contracts.

**That seems to be why writing was first invented, about 8000 years ago in the Middle East.**

## 2 Writing versus speech

Of the three main methods of communication – visual, spoken and written – written communication is the one we acquired most recently, and it's still the one we need to work hardest at. Children learn to use their eyes and to speak their language without any great difficulty, but learning to write is always a struggle. That's why most people, in most situations, prefer to use speech rather than writing to send their messages, and prefer to receive them by listening or looking at images rather than reading.

There are obviously some situations when it is vital to speak – and when it would be stupid to write. For example, if there was a bomb warning and you had to evacuate the building, it would not be wise to inform your workteam by pinning up a notice.

Here are some more situations where speaking would be better:

- when you want to ask someone the time;
- when someone in your workteam asks for help;
- when your views are requested at a meeting;
- when you're asked for a personal opinion 'off the record';
- when you're showing someone how to perform a task.

## Activity 1

*2 mins*

Think about the situations I have just described. What can you say in general about the situations where speech is better than writing?

_____

_____

_____

You may have put it differently, but I hope you would agree with me that there are three kinds of situation where speech is definitely the better choice:

- when you need to communicate immediately;
- when the person you need to reach is readily available;
- when there is no need to put your words on record.

If you don't have to write, there is no point in doing so, because in general speech has three advantages over writing:

> Speech is quicker, but writing may save you time in the long run.

- it is more immediate;
- it can have more impact;
- speaking is a lot quicker than writing.

With so much modern technology available, the written word has been gaining ground, but research into what managers do shows that while they spend up to two-thirds of their time communicating (in meetings or listening and talking to individuals), two-thirds of this time is spent listening. Only a small amount of their time is spent reading or writing.

Nevertheless writing has many uses, and some important advantages. I will use a few examples to show what I mean. The first example is notes of an incident.

■ Don witnessed a nasty accident in the hospital canteen's delivery bay. Two women employees were hurt when the tailgate of a lorry came unfastened. As soon as they had been taken around to Casualty, the Catering Services Manager called Don into her office, and after checking that he was personally all right, she asked him what he had seen. While Don talked, she took notes. When he had finished she said 'Right, Don. Nasty business. You'd better get all that down in writing now.'

There is more on notes in Session C.

## Activity 2

*2 mins*

What will be the advantages of having Don's statement in writing? Make a note of **two** advantages.

_____

_____

Evidence will be needed because there might well be a formal investigation by the Health and Safety Executive; at the very least, the two injured employees will probably want to claim compensation, and the case may go to a Tribunal. (There is also a legal requirement to enter this kind of incident in the Accident Book, but that is a separate matter.)

Human memory fades, and as time passes we become less and less able to recall events accurately; so it makes sense to get the facts down in writing at the first opportunity. Don's statement will be filed and used at a later date, and may be circulated to a number of different locations.

We can sum up the advantages of a written statement by saying:

■ it creates a **permanent record**;
■ it is more likely to be **accurate** than anyone's memory;
■ it can **cross both time and space** to be used again.

The second example is a discussion paper.

- Manjit had been reporting problems with a particular supplier since the beginning of the year. The purchasing committee was due to meet in a fortnight's time, and Manjit was asked to submit a full report about the problems that had occurred, giving precise details of dates, materials involved and any correspondence that had taken place. 'It needs to be completely accurate, so check your facts carefully', she was told. 'Your report will be the basis for deciding whether or not we go on using them.'

## Activity 3

3 mins

What were the advantages of having Manjit put her information in writing? Make a note of **two** advantages.

_____

_____

_____

A less efficient committee would just have asked Manjit to come along and tell them about the problems. However, this is an important business matter, and it is not wise to rely on a verbal account alone as:

- it is likely to be incomplete;
- hard facts and definite evidence may be lacking;
- personal bias may creep in.

It is far better to ask for a written report, giving Manjit time to dig up facts, dates and copies of letters, and to send copies of the report to committee members in advance of the meeting.

They can then think about it beforehand, and prepare their questions and comments. Manjit can also be invited to attend the meeting, to answer these questions and add her own views. This is businesslike, fair and efficient.

So the advantages of having a written report in advance are:

- it should provide a complete and detailed record of the facts;
- it should be reliable and credible, because there is time to prepare it properly;
- it can cross time and space to form the basis of a later discussion.

The third example is a quick reference card.

■ In Marie's section of a large mail-order firm, labour turnover was high, and a lot of Marie's time was taken up with giving newly recruited telephone clerks basic training in the correct procedures. These took time to sink in, and the clerks frequently made mistakes, or got stuck, and had to call on Marie to help.

Marie decided to deal with this by listing the main points of each task on sheets of card, and giving a set to each clerk after the initial training session. She told them to refer to the cards when they weren't sure what to do, and only to come back to her if there was a major problem. It took her several hours to work out what the key points should be, and how to put them, but she felt the effort was worth it.

## Activity 4

3 mins

What would be the advantages of using a 'quick reference card' rather than telling staff what to do? Make a note of **two** advantages.

_____

_____

Marie and her clerks were wasting a lot of time when she relied on spoken instructions only. Using her new cards meant that inexperienced clerks made fewer mistakes and wasted less of Marie's time.

The advantages of writing in this example are:

■ it saves time and money;
■ it helps new recruits learn the job more quickly;
■ it ensures consistency, because everyone has the same instructions.

The final example is the minutes of a meeting.

■ When Steve read the minutes of the monthly Management meeting he saw he was reported as saying 'There is no question of anyone from my team being sent on the Advanced Course as they do not have the intellectual ability.' He argued with the secretary: 'That's wrong. I didn't say that!' but when he was asked whether his own notes of the meeting showed something different, he had to admit he hadn't made any. The secretary declined to change the minutes, though in the minutes of the next meeting, he did let Steve add a comment to the effect that 'he might have been hasty in his judgement'.

## Activity 5

3 mins

What are the advantages of having written minutes to record what was said at a meeting? Make a note of **two** advantages.

_____

_____

Dr Jones was absolutely fed up with his patient, Mrs W. One day he wrote on her file 'this woman is a complete idiot!' On her next visit, she happened to see the file — and promptly made a formal complaint to the Family Health Authority!

'Minutes' are really only notes, though they are accurate and rather formal notes. They are essential for keeping track of what happened in earlier meetings, and for passing on views, facts and decisions. In committees, many people may speak, complicated arguments may arise and there may be disagreements. The committee must have an accurate record.

So the advantages of having written minutes are that:

■ they provide an accurate record of past meetings;
■ they can contain as much detail as needed (though it's a bad mistake to put in too much detail)
■ they cross space and time to inform and guide other people's actions.

There are some other lessons from this example: it pays to make your own notes of what happens at meetings, in case a disagreement arises later. And where formal minutes are being taken it pays to think before you speak!

# 3 The advantages of writing

The main practical difference between speech and writing is that speech is temporary. Like the ripples on a pond, speech soon fades away without a trace. Speech is fine for getting immediate action and communicating small amounts of information, but it is very ineffective when:

- the speaker tries to communicate too much information;
- the listeners have to remember it for too long.

Human beings generally are not very good at listening and remembering. We often mis-hear, and misinterpret what we hear, and we have only a limited capacity for absorbing information through our ears. Too much, and it simply goes 'over our heads'.

We do have a large capacity for memory, but it is unreliable.

We remember some things all our lives, but a lot of what we hear and read fails to stick. As time passes, memories can crumble and fade, and get hopelessly muddled.

Writing can overcome these problems – and it serves some other uses too.

## 3.1 Writing as memory

The written word is a massive improvement on human memory – we use books, manuals, reports and all sorts of other documents to store information for future reference. Reference libraries and computer databases are memory substitutes on a vast scale (indeed, we often refer to 'computer memory'). But when you write a short confidential report on a member of your workteam, and someone in Personnel puts it in a file, that is basically the same process.

Writing can provide a permanent and reliable record of large amounts of detailed information which can be used for future reference.

## 3.2 Writing can cross time and space

Speech is best for a 'live' audience in the here-and-now. But writing can cross unlimited distances in space and distances in time.

Distance in time is really about the permanent record, or memory, aspect of writing. Once something is in writing, preserving it is fairly simple. Although many of the documents that you write at work will only have a limited life, and will be thrown away after a few weeks, others can have a much longer life.

**7**

# Activity 6

Make a note of a few things you have recently written at work which will probably still exist somewhere, in someone else's files if not in yours, in a year's time.

_____

_____

_____

_____

If your job involves a lot of paperwork, then scores of things you have written will probably still be on file in a year's time. I certainly keep notes of meetings, copies of letters, and even time sheets, checklists and costings – and often for many years.

This is a good reason for trying to write well: some complete stranger may be reading through your words in ten years' time!

Writing also helps us communicate across distance in space – from site to site, town to town, and even from country to country.

EXTENSION I
A list of the advantages and disadvantages of fax and e-mail as channels of communication. It would be helpful to read this now.

Of course, if the messages are urgent, simple and short, it may be better to speak across these distances on the phone. Many people now have the option of sending such short and urgent messages either by fax or by electronic mail. This is communication in writing, but with something approaching the greater immediacy of the phone call. Fax stands for facsimile, a device that transmits and receives documents via the telephone network. Electronic mail or e-mail is a system for sending very fast and accurate messages between computers using electronic transmission.

Certainly, where the messages are less urgent, but longer and more detailed, you need to write them down, or at least write 'back-up' notes to remind you of the circumstances. It is often wise to note the time, date and other details when:

- you received an important message;
- a particular problem arose;
- you had a bright idea;
- you witnessed an incident of some kind.

## Activity 7

*2 mins*

Make a note of some of the things which you have to communicate, in writing, over substantial distances:

_____

_____

_____

_____

In my case, in the last few days, I have had to send several written communications across the distance barrier:

- a ten-page report on a new training course, faxed to a company ninety miles away;
- a batch of survey questionnaires, posted to an office thirty miles away;
- a copy of a formal contract to an organization in Brussels.

> Writing is ideal for communicating lots of detail — but if there's too much, no one will want to read it!

None of these could have been communicated satisfactorily in speech over the phone – there was simply too much detail. Actually, I did phone, but mainly to let the 'other side' know that the documents were on their way, and in the first case to give them the gist of what the report was saying.

# 3.3 Written documents can easily be copied

Another big advantage of written communications is that they can easily be copied – and copied exactly.

When you need to reach a large number of people all at the same time and with an identical message, the answer is simple: put your message in writing and copy it.

- Clinton Rollers Ltd needed to recall a faulty product. They checked their customer files and sent a standard letter to all 500 customers who had bought the product. The customers thus received an identical message, which was guaranteed to contain all the relevant information. This also had the benefit of being much cheaper and more convenient than making 500 phone calls.

## 3.4 Writing as back-up

I do not want to give the impression that there is an 'either–or' choice between writing and speaking. As some of the examples showed, the best way to communicate may often be a combination of the two.

## Activity 8

5 mins

■ Callie held a briefing session to explain to her workteam the new proposals for flexible working hours. At the end of the session she handed each of them a sheet of paper listing the main points of the proposal:

**Flexible working hours**

1 In any four-week period you should work an average of 140 hours.
2 Daily hours can be worked between 8.00 a.m. and 6.00 p.m.
3 Up to ten hours' credit or debit can be carried forward to the next four-week period.
4 Core time (11.00 a.m. to 3.00 p.m.) should be worked daily unless you are taking holiday or credit hours carried forward.
5 Hours to be worked daily should normally be arranged one week in advance, in co-operation with your supervisor, and workteam.

What would you say are the benefits of giving the workteam this list, and letting them take it away with them afterwards?

I think the main benefit is simply putting it on the record. As I have already said, most people aren't good listeners, and memories are unreliable. It is common for a group of people to come away from a verbal briefing with entirely different ideas about what was said and what was meant. Later, when they start to discuss the briefing among themselves, the 'story' will inevitably get even more muddled and inaccurate.

Giving them a written document will prevent confusion, because it ensures that everyone gets the same information.

Certainly, it will give rise to many questions, but at least everyone concerned has a written basis for that discussion, which will help keep it on the rails.

Writing and speech come together in 'discussion papers' — where someone writes down some ideas to give a focus for talking about the issues.

## 3.5 Writing to pass on a message

There is a party game called 'ghosts' or 'Chinese whispers', where the first person whispers a message to the next, who whispers it to the next, and so on. The point of the game is to see how mangled the message can get by the time it reaches the end of the chain.

This is how 'Send reinforcements, we're going to advance' ends up as 'Send three and fourpence, we're going to a dance' – and exactly the same thing can happen in reality when someone takes a verbal message for you and verbally passes it on in a mangled or incomplete form. This can cause a lot of damage, nuisance and expense, as this example shows.

■ Alan is in the office at 12.45 p.m., when the telephone rings. It's Shar-Day Printers Ltd wanting to speak to Brendan, who is out, about a delivery of litho plates that they should have received three days ago. They can't afford to wait more than another 24 hours. If delivery can't be guaranteed in that time, they'll cancel the order and go elsewhere.

Alan goes off to meet another customer at 1.00 p.m. and asks the typist in the next office to keep an eye open for Brendan and tell him to phone the customer. When Brendan gets back at 1.30 p.m., she simply tells him 'someone phoned about an order'.

He is a busy man, with a lot of urgent jobs to do, and the message doesn't sound all that important. Brendan does nothing.

Next morning an angry fax arrives cancelling the order and demanding to know why no-one has phoned back.

---

## Activity 9

5 mins

What should Alan have done to make sure that Brendan dealt with the problem? At least **three** things are involved.

_____

_____

_____

If Alan took responsibility for answering the phone, he should also have taken responsibility for ensuring that the message got through to Brendan – and that Brendan understood it.

He couldn't relay the message directly to Brendan, who wasn't there. But he could easily have written it.

In fact, he should have made a written note while the person from Shar-Day was talking to him. Then when they rang off, he should have:

- rewritten it neatly and checked that all the details were included;
- marked it 'URGENT';
- put it where Brendan was bound to see it;
- checked later to see that he had done so.

That is no doubt what you would like your colleagues to do for you – so make sure you do it for them!

# 3.6 Writing as a legal requirement

Finally, there are some situations where we need to put something in writing:

- because the law requires it;
- in order to protect ourselves if the law does get involved.

## Activity 10

*4 mins*

What sorts of things are you required by law to put in writing, as part of your responsibilities at work?

_____

_____

_____

_____

_____

Obviously this will vary a great deal, but depending on what job you do, and how wide your responsibilities are, you might have to write, or draft for approval:

- entries in the accident book;
- statutory warning notices;
- statutory certificates and authorizations;
- statements required by police or courts;
- documents for Tribunals;
- various legal documents, especially if you work in banking, finance or some aspect of the law.

There are also situations where employees are entitled by law to have something in writing (even if it isn't you personally who has to provide it) including:

The fact that you need to write something for legal reasons doesn't mean you have to write in 'legalese': always try to keep it plain and simple.

- a written statement of terms and conditions of employment;
- a statement of the employer's health and safety policy;
- notification of changes in contractual terms;
- an explanation of deductions from pay.

But the biggest area where the law needs to be considered is all those situations where you are not legally required to put something in writing, but where it is a good idea to do so for your own protection – those 'covering your back' situations.

This includes anything where one day you may need to be able to prove what you did and what you said, so:

- if you refuse an **instruction** (or someone refuses an instruction from you), make a note of the time, the circumstances and what precisely happened;
- if you receive or reply to a **complaint** from outside the organization, put it in writing and keep a copy;
- if you write any document with **legal implications**, keep a copy;
- if an **unusual incident** occurs, note down the details.

It is particularly important to make a note of anything you say or do that **may affect another employee's legal rights**. Remember too that the law on race and sex discrimination applies to people's treatment in respect of matters as diverse as promotion, access to training, holiday allocation, disciplinary measures and allocation of work.

# 3.7 Analysing your written communication needs

I don't want you to think that you should spend all your time on paperwork, or that you have to record every little thing that happens. No doubt most of the time you will continue to communicate in speech.

But I hope you can see now that there are quite a lot of situations where:

- either you should write rather than speak;
- or you should back up what you say in writing.

It is simply a matter of using your common sense. Next time you are wondering how to get your message through most effectively, just pause for a moment and ask yourself:

- 'Would it be better to put this in writing?'
- 'Should I use writing to back up my words?'

And whenever something happens which is out of the ordinary, ask yourself:

- 'Would it be a good idea to make a note of that?'

Finally, although writing takes more time and trouble than saying something out loud, even in this computerized age, always ask yourself:

- 'Will I save a lot more time and trouble later, if I take the time and trouble to put it in writing now?'

# Activity 11

25
mins

**This Activity may provide the basis of appropriate evidence for your S/NVQ portfolio. If you are intending to take this course of action, it might be better to write your answers on separate sheets of paper.**

It will be useful to try to analyse what you write over a period of, say, a week, under the following headings:

■ **What?**

i.e. memo, notice, note, report, leaflet, letter, handwritten note, file note, etc.

■ **To whom?**

i.e. customer, staff, colleague, boss, team, general public, supplier, etc.; to one person or copied to several

■ **Why?**

i.e. to answer a request or inquiry, to warn, advise, inform, remind, request action or information, to put something on the record, etc.

■ **How?**

internal mail, external post, fax, e-mail, etc.

■ **Response?**

i.e. if the communication required a response, did you get it?

You should draw up several sheets of paper with these headings, and log every item that you send out, apart from routine forms (we will say something about these in Session D).

When you have collected a week's worth of items, sit back and consider them.

■ What are the **three** most common kinds of item?
■ Who do they most commonly go to?
■ Are you getting the results you would like?
■ Which items do you find most challenging?

Use these questions to work out ways of improving your written output. (You will also find it valuable to talk to a more experienced colleague about the quality and effectiveness of your written communications, and the impression that they create.)

# Self-assessment 1

8 mins

You may wish to re-read Extension 1 before answering question 6.

1  In the seven situations below, say whether writing, speech, or both or either would be the best way to communicate your messages.

a  When a member of your team wants advice about a work problem. _____

b  When a matter of legal significance may be involved. _____

c  It is an emergency and you need action to be taken immediately. _____

d  You need to communicate the same message to large numbers of people. _____

e  You need to send your message across time and space. _____

f  You need to communicate with people at a different location. _____

g  You want to put forward some proposals for discussion at a committee. _____

2  Complete the following statements with a suitable word or group of words.

a  Writing is the best choice if you need to put your words on _____.

b  Communicating in _____ can be very ineffective when too much _____ is involved and the listeners have to _____ it for too long.

c  An important advantage of communicating in _____ is that you can get exactly the _____ message to a large number of people.

3  Give **four** examples of situations where it would be useful to note the time, date and other details:

_____

_____

_____

_____

**15**

4 What is 'fax' short for?

_____

5 When you are taking part in a meeting that is being minuted, why does it pay to think before you speak?

_____

6 State **one** advantage and **one** disadvantage of communicating by:

a Fax.

_____

_____

b Electronic mail (e-mail).

_____

_____

Answers to these questions can be found on pages 94–5.

# 5 Summary

- Writing is preferable to speaking when:

  - the communication needs to cross distances in space and time;
  - it needs to be put on record (for example for legal reasons);
  - the record needs to be accurate;
  - it contains large amounts of information;
  - a back-up to spoken messages is needed;
  - a reliable basis for later discussion is needed;
  - a consistent message needs to be sent to several people.

- Some things are required by law to be in writing.

- Messages passed from person to person in speech are unreliable: it's best to write them down.

- When you have the choice of whether to speak, to write, or both, you should ask yourself the following:

  - Would it be better to put this in writing?
  - Should I use writing to back up what I have said?
  - Would it be a good idea to make a note of that?
  - Will I save a lot of time and trouble later, if I take the time and trouble to put this in writing now?

# Session B  Writing for results

## 1  Introduction

The first rule for successful communicating is to give it a bit of thought. You should ask yourself:

- Who do I need to communicate with?
- What result do I want to achieve?
- What impression do I want to give?

Apart from 'self-communication' (private diaries, personal notes, records placed on file, and so on) all communication is designed:

- to reach some other person;
- to achieve a result.

The result – the purpose – may be to ask, order or persuade the other person to do something; or it may be to provide them with information. Either way, the end result will be action of some kind.

We can make a diagram of all this as follows:

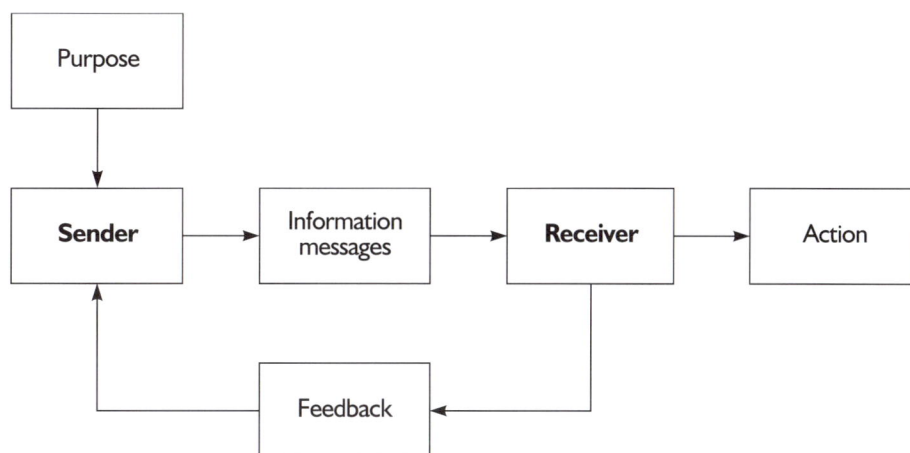

```
      ┌──────────┐
      │ Purpose  │
      └────┬─────┘
           │
           ▼
┌────────┐   ┌─────────────┐   ┌──────────┐   ┌────────┐
│ Sender │──▶│ Information  │──▶│ Receiver │──▶│ Action │
│        │   │  messages    │   │          │   │        │
└───▲────┘   └─────────────┘   └────┬─────┘   └────────┘
    │                                │
    │         ┌──────────┐           │
    └─────────│ Feedback │◀──────────┘
              └──────────┘
```

Often, as this diagram suggests, there is an exchange of some kind: the receiver becomes a sender, and feeds back information to the sender of the original message.

The trouble with communication is that these days there is an awful lot of it going on. If you want your communications to achieve the desired results, you need to do everything you can to make sure that:

- they reach their destination;
- the receiver notices them;
- the receiver understands and acts on them.

Some people are a lot more successful at communicating than others. In this part of the workbook, we'll see why and how.

# 2 Reaching the destination

Whenever you are communicating in writing, your first priority should be to ensure that your message actually reaches its destination.

When facsimile transmission (to give 'fax' its full name) was introduced in the early 1980s, receiving a fax was a rarity. When one arrived it was always given a high priority and rushed to the addressee. Nowadays faxing is so commonplace and routine that faxed documents are much more likely to be mislaid or ignored.

- For example, Suraj was asked to prepare a bid for County Council funds to allow the Multi-Racial Educational Resource Centre to open four evenings a week instead of two. He drew up what he thought was a very convincing case, and faxed the document through to the Equality Committee on 21 June, two days before the deadline.

A fortnight later, having heard nothing, Suraj phoned the committee secretary to ask if his bid had been considered. The secretary knew nothing about it: the document had gone astray, and since the deadline was now past, the bid could not be considered.

The fax is an important channel of communication, but it has its drawbacks. For example, when someone sends a fax it does tend to disappear into an electronic void. Did it go to the right number? Did it get through at all? Did it reach the right person? A really important letter can always be posted by recorded delivery, with a guarantee of arrival, but this isn't the case with the fax.

# Activity 12

2 mins

How could Suraj have ensured that his bid got through to the right person?

_____

_____

_____

When the document is both important and urgent, it's worth making the effort to check. I think that if I had been in Suraj's position:

- before sending the fax, I would have checked that the number faxed was correct, and afterwards checked that transmission went ahead without errors;
- I would have telephoned the committee secretary in advance

  a  to notify him that the document was coming;
  b  to check the fax number;
  c  to ask for confirmation of receipt;

- if I hadn't heard anything by, say, the day before the deadline, I would have phoned to check whether the document had arrived.

Where a fax is confidential, it may be wise to ask the person to whom it is being sent to stand by to receive it personally.

**EXTENSION 1**
For a summary of the advantages and disadvantages of fax and e-mail.

The lessons are these:

- make sure that your documents are clearly and correctly addressed;
- send them by a suitably reliable channel;
- use a guaranteed delivery method for high-priority documents;
- if necessary, check that they have actually arrived.

Even if it's just a matter of pinning a note on a noticeboard, it always pays to check that it's reaching the intended audience.

## 3  Getting the reader's attention

The best starting point is to put yourself in the shoes of the person you are trying to reach.

## Activity 13

5 mins

You are short of time, and you probably have a lot of written material to deal with.

When a document, letter, note or memo reaches you, it places more demands on your time. What can the sender do to make your task easier?

Jot down **three** or **four** ideas.

_____

_____

_____

_____

If the sender is thinking about the receiver's needs (your needs) there are two main things he or she can do.

The first is to make it as easy as possible for you to:

- identify who sent it and what it is about;
- decide whether it is important or not.

The second is to make it as easy as possible for you to:

- read it, if important;
- work out what it is saying;
- decide what action you need to take as a result.

The easier you make it, the more likely the receiver is to read it, and the more likely you are to achieve your objectives. What makes it easier? I would say:

- keeping it as short as possible;
- using plain and simple language;
- making the 'key messages' – especially when you are requesting action of some kind – as visible as possible;
- laying the document out so that it's easy to read.

> Managers often have problems dealing with the flood of incoming material. They need to be able to prioritize quickly: do I read it now, read it later, file it or 'bin' it?

One of the biggest problems for anyone with responsibilities is the blizzard of paperwork they receive. We suffer from 'information overload': so much information and so many communications are flying around all the time that it's very hard to decide what's significant and what isn't.

Here's an example of a communication that really helps the reader:

| | |
|---|---|
| To | R. Marley<br>Disputed Claims Manager |
| From | Richard Longman<br>*Region 12 Household claims section team leader* |
| Subject | <u>Investigation into claim by Ms Z. Pallavicini</u><br><br>This note explains why we were suspicious, how the claim was investigated, and the action I think should be taken.<br><br>I would be grateful if you could let me have your decision by 18 February. |
| Attachment | Summary claim report |

From the receiver's point of view, nothing could be clearer – even down to knowing when the decision needs to be made by!

Many organizations use standard layouts for documents such as letters, reports, memos, faxes and e-mails in order to make it as easy as possible for readers to identify them. However, there might perhaps be a disadvantage in standardizing everything. Can you think of one?

_____

_____

Suppose your particular memo is very urgent, and you want it to go straight to the top of the pile, but you will have to compete with lots of other identical-looking documents. How can you make your document stand out?

I'll leave you to think of some ways you could do so without breaking any of the accepted rules of your organization. But there is a word of warning: one organization I know always heads its faxes with the words 'VERY, VERY URGENT' in big black letters. To begin with, this gets them priority, but after you have received three or four of these, the headline starts to lose its power, and you ending up treating these messages exactly like all the rest.

# 3.1 Keeping it short and simple

There are two issues here:

- what you say;
- and how you say it.

What you say depends on thinking about what the receiver needs to know. It's counter-productive to say too little: the receiver will be unable to use the information properly, and will come back for more details, which will double the amount of time you've had to spend on the matter. On the other hand, if you say too much, you're wasting both your own time and the receiver's.

- The note by Richard Longman to the Disputed Claims Manager dealt with quite a complicated subject. The company suspected the customer of having made a fraudulent claim, and this has been investigated.

Richard Longman has a whole file on the case, containing dozens of memos, reports, notes and copies of forms. However, the Disputed Claims Manager didn't need to know all that. He or she simply needed an accurate and factual summary. After all, the complete file will still be there if anything needs double-checking.

Richard decided to include the following information:

Remember to KISS:
Keep It Short and
Simple!

- the claimant's full name and address;
- the policy number and date;
- the date of the claim;
- the nature and value of the claim;
- who processed it, and when;
- why it aroused suspicion;
- what action was then taken, and when;
- how it was investigated, and by whom;
- dates of any interviews or correspondence with the claimant that formed part of the investigation;
- the investigator's conclusions.

# Activity 15

3 mins

I think it would make sense for Richard Longman's organization to use a standard form for reports of this kind. What advantages do you think that would bring?

_____

_____

_____

_____

Three possible advantages of using standard forms occurred to me:

- the structure and layout of the forms would soon become familiar, so both filling them in and reading them would be easier;
- it would save the sender having to decide what information to include;
- it would ensure that the sender didn't forget to cover all the important points.

The sender could still write a covering note to explain any additional issues, to make reservations or to stress particular points.

**The key messages**

After Activity 13 we said that one of three things that would make the recipient's task easier is setting out the 'key messages'. These might also be included in a slot on the standard form, but if Richard wished to include them in a written document, he would probably have headed them clearly, as follows.

| | |
|---|---|
| Conclusions | Mrs Pallavicini is a comparatively new customer, and there were reasonable grounds for being suspicious about her claim. |
| | However, no firm evidence of fraud could be found, and the Investigation Department believes that the police would not consider that the case justifies a criminal investigation. |
| Recommendations: | 1 To pay the claim in full<br>2 To decline to insure this claimant in future. |

Short and to the point: indeed, there is a strong case for starting the document with these conclusions.

Depending on the time available, the recipient can now:

- act immediately on this information;
- or review the accompanying forms or 'narrative' before doing so;
- or go back to the original file to check details and clarify any queries.

To return to our starting point, this kind of approach:

- saves the reader time and mental effort;
- simplifies decision making;
- minimizes the need to spend time on clarification and queries (each of which can result in another tedious and unnecessary round of paperwork).

It's good to send communications of this quality: it is efficient from the organization's point of view, and it gets the sender a good reputation for competence and clear thinking.

## 3.2 The ABC of effective written communication

Accuracy, brevity and clarity are the ABC of effective written communication.

- Accuracy:

  - get the facts right;
  - use correct grammar and spelling.

- Brevity:

  - stick to the point;
  - don't use more words than you need to.

- Clarity:

  - express yourself simply and clearly;
  - use a logical structure.

**23**

I am not going to say anything about getting the facts right, except to say that it is up to you to prepare and check them before you commit yourself to writing. Remember that writing can go on the record for a very long time: if you have made a silly factual mistake it will not be easy to get rid of it. We will come back to grammar and spelling shortly.

# 4 Plain words

In written communication it is almost always better to use simple and straightforward language, especially if you are dealing with practical and straightforward people.

Here is an example of someone who seems incapable of being straightforward.

---

**MEMORANDUM**

**To:**       Belinda Wasserman, Production

**From:**     Tom Robinson, Customer Services

**Subject:**  <u>Recent developments</u>

You asked me to comment on the problems we have been experiencing recently with regard to maintaining adequate inventory for meeting agreed performance criteria for meeting customer orders for made-up fabrics for the mail-order market.

Our position is already well known. There have been extreme difficulties in the recent period and this has had negative effects particularly in terms of customer complaints. These are up by a considerable margin of late.

Regarding quality we have not become aware of any substantial variation from the normal picture.

Finally, packaging standards appear to be experiencing some degree of deterioration as more has come back as damaged in the post.

Fabric-based motor accessories do not appear to present a problem as at this moment in time.

---

Remember your ABC: Accurate, Brief and Clear

# 4.1 Short words or long?

There are all sorts of things wrong with the way this memo is written. For example, the first paragraph wouldn't have been necessary at all if he had used an informative title for the memo.

However, I want to concentrate on the words and phrases Tom uses.

In the English language there are many different ways of saying things, and there are long and short alternatives for a lot of ideas. In the passage above, we could replace long words with short ones as follows:

| Long | Short |
|---|---|
| developments | events |
| experiencing | having, seeing |
| maintaining | keeping |
| negative | bad |
| regarding | as for |
| considerable | large, big |
| substantial | large, big |
| variation | change |

Some of the long words in this passage are not so easily shortened, because they are in effect 'technical terms', and have a specific meaning that is not easy to reproduce in ordinary language:

> performance criteria
> deterioration
> accessories

'Inventory' is a borderline case; it means 'stocks', but in many organizations people are used to the longer word.

Clearly, if you can use shorter words which have the same meaning, you are likely to make your writing easier to understand.

# Activity 16

8 mins

Write down **one** or **two** short words which could replace the long ones in the list below. I have done the first two for you.

| Long | Short |
|------|-------|
| advantageous | useful |
| application | use |
| ascertain | _____ |
| commencement | _____ |
| comprehension | _____ |
| consequently | _____ |
| deficiency | _____ |
| disadvantage | _____ |
| elucidate | _____ |
| emphasize | _____ |
| excessive | _____ |
| expedite | _____ |
| expenditure | _____ |
| fundamental | _____ |
| furthermore | _____ |
| illustrate | _____ |
| inventory | _____ |
| relationship | _____ |
| subsequently | _____ |
| terminate | _____ |
| unprecedented | _____ |
| utilization | _____ |

Answers can be found on page 99.

**26**

'He's a man of few words', said the Research Director's secretary, 'It just so happens that they're all incredibly long'.

Thus instead of saying something like:

'Subsequently we comprehended the fundamental disadvantages of excessive expenditure on inventory.'

we can say:

'Later we grasped the basic drawbacks of spending too much on stocks.'

The problem is not just with individual words, but with whole phrases.

# Activity 17

*3 mins*

Suppose you received the following letter:

■ Dear Sir

With reference to your recent letter, we are now in a position to advise you that your order has been expedited and you should obtain receipt of the outstanding goods, namely 24 HP 8MB SIMM cards, by 31 January latest.

Assuring you of our best attention at all times,

Yours faithfully

_____

Jot down what you think about the way the letter is written.

_____
_____
_____
_____

What impression do you form of the writer from reading the letter?

_____
_____
_____
_____

(Don't bother about the possible inefficiency which led to the letter being necessary in the first place.)

Well, I think the first thing to strike you would be the unnatural and old-fashioned language used: 'We are now in a position to advise you' and 'you should obtain receipt' are just two examples.

We understand what the writer is saying, but he or she could have said it far more simply. For example 'you should receive', or 'the order should arrive' would be better than 'you should obtain receipt'. And 'we are now in a position to advise you', could probably have been left out altogether if the sentence had been changed a little.

But worse than this, the writer uses one word, 'expedited', which quite possibly the reader wouldn't understand. In fact, it means 'hurried up', nothing more, but you suspect that the writer is using it to sound important and official.

Trying to make ourselves sound important is an understandable human weakness but it doesn't usually cut much ice! A letter like this is more likely to annoy or amuse its readers than impress them.

Finally, the writer uses some flowery phrases which once used to be very common in commercial writing, but which have now largely been abandoned. Beginning a letter 'with reference to' tends to involve you in writing a very cumbersome sentence. It's simpler and sounds better to deal with what you are referring to in a separate sentence like this: 'Thank you for your recent letter. I have followed up your order . . .'. And 'Assuring you of our best attention at all times', although it sounds friendly enough, could well be replaced by something simpler like: 'We apologize for the delay', in the example we've been looking at.

I have two other complaints about this letter:

- it fails to identify the particular order or its date, both of which are important when talking about matters of this kind;
- it is horribly impersonal.

# 4.2 Long-winded phrases

Simple phrases, as well as simple words, are often better, but long-winded ways of saying things are all too common. 'Clichés' are a special problem: because we hear and read them so often, they are frequently the first expressions that come to mind.

Here are a few examples of what I mean with a simpler alternative shown alongside them.

| | |
|---|---|
| with regard to | *about* |
| a large proportion of | *many* |
| at an early date | *soon* |
| at the present moment in time | *currently/now* |
| in consequence of | *because of/owing to* |
| due to the fact that | *because of/owing to* |

If we try putting these expressions in sentences we can see that the simpler alternative puts the idea across more effectively and saves time and energy for the writer and the reader.

## Activity 18

Here are some more examples of sentences containing long-winded, overworked expressions which can be replaced by simpler, clearer ones. Jot down what you think would be a better word to use in each of these sentences instead of the group of words highlighted.

**Despite the fact that** deliveries of raw materials were late, the order was met on time.

_____

This **in many cases** proved to be so.

_____

I should like to **draw your attention to the fact** that I haven't been paid.

_____

We must **give due consideration to** the staff development programme.

_____

**In view of the fact that** I am retiring this year, I **am of the opinion that** somebody else should undertake the long-term project.

_____

_____

All departments, **with the exception of** Data Processing, were represented.

_____

Here are my suggestions, though other words would do as well in some cases. I've written the whole sentence out each time so that you can see that using a simpler expression improves the sentence and doesn't affect the meaning in any way.

- Although deliveries of raw materials were late, the order was met on time.
- This often proved to be so (or: This was often so.)
- I should like to point out that I haven't been paid.
- We must consider the staff development programme.
- Since I am retiring this year, I feel that somebody else should undertake the long-term project.
- All departments except Data Processing were represented.

**29**

If we were writing a checklist for 'How to Make Your Writing as Long-Winded as Possible' we could say:

- don't think for yourself, use whatever wordy expressions are current (and don't worry too much about the meaning);
- if one word will do, use six.

When you write simply your ideas and decisions come across simply and honestly. Be on your guard for people who try to disguise the truth of what they are saying by wrapping things up in a blanket of words to confuse the reader.

# 4.3  Watch out for 'jargon'

It's very easy to slip into using jargon, which means special words and phrases that one person is familiar with, but others aren't. Training specialists, for example, talk about competences, performance criteria, self-assessment, 'cloze exercises', opportunity costs and so on. Other specialists know exactly what they mean, but 'outsiders' usually don't.

Technical aspects of the job also produce a lot of jargon, like the reference to 'HP 8MB SIMMs' in the letter we looked at on page 27. In this case both writer and reader knew what was meant (these are 8-megabyte computer memory chips for Hewlett-Packard laser printers), but you can't always rely on this.

## Activity 19
6 mins

Another kind of jargon is 'management-speak', a special kind of language that is intended to put a pseudo-scientific 'spin' on unpleasant realities. Here is an example:

Downsizing typically generates negative trends in employee motivation, focused on perceptions of disempowerment and fuelled by inadequately managed 'information-creep'.

Try rewriting this short passage in simple language — if you can work out what it means!

_____

_____

_____

_____

At Question Time, the Prime Minister said: 'Do you agree the government should not sit in a boardroom, in a metaphysical sense?' (7 Feb 96) He meant 'in a metaphorical sense'; look the two words up to see what they mean.

I would write the passage something like this:

Job cuts usually lower morale, especially when they leave staff feeling helpless and there are lots of rumours flying around.

That puts a rather different complexion on it, doesn't it?

There's another point to watch with this kind of thing: if you try to use a lot of long, impressive-sounding words you may end up using one you don't understand, and get it wrong. That could be embarrassing.

## 4.4  An issue of quality

In organizations that have a strong focus on quality, written communications have an important role to play.

For example, quality may be judged in a number of ways, depending for instance on whether:

- you provide information that is accurate, complete, and timely;
- your written communications to customers (both internal and external) are polite, pleasant and 'human';
- you classify and store your written records correctly;
- your communications, whatever their purpose, are designed to be understandable as well as technically accurate.

## 5  Making the right impression

Clarity, accuracy, simplicity and humanity in your writing will help you get better results. You will find it easier to reach your target, and the receiver will be more likely to read, understand and act upon your words.

It will also boost your own reputation, because although your written communications are intended to achieve some purpose, they are also about human relationships. When you send someone a communication, you are also sending images and impressions about yourself, whether you intend to or not, and whether the receiver is conscious of them or not.

# 5.1 Writing styles

Here is an example, addressed to you. Read it carefully; and then think about what impression you get of the sender.

P.F. Wapentake
Head of Resourcing Policy Research
Resourcing Policy Unit
Business Development Services
Cramley Research Institute
Cramley University

Dear Sir or Madam

As Head of Resourcing Policy Research I have pleasure in sending you a copy of the Resource Policy Unit's report on trends and developments in controlled and limited-list tendering procedures, as defined in the European Union Procurement Directives (cumulative annualizing provisions).

Regrettably the Unit is not in a position to answer any enquiries relating to the research. However, if your organization wishes to submit any evidence for consideration under the ongoing review process you should write to G.O. Scorse, Deputy Head of Resourcing Policy Research, at the above address. Such contributions will not be acknowledged.

Yours faithfully

## Activity 20

*3 mins*

Write down briefly what impression you get about the person who wrote this letter, and what kind of relationship is likely to be created between sender and receiver.

This communication is as dull as ditchwater, and although Wapentake invites you to respond, the letter seems designed to make sure that you do not! Your most likely response is to 'bin' the whole thing.

The writer comes across as a colourless but self-important person who is going through the motions of communicating without having any genuine interest in the outcome.

## Activity 21

*15 mins*

Look through some of the written communications you have sent out recently. Think about how you 'come over' to your readers.

Below is a series of scales on which you can rate the impression you give.

For example, if you think you come over as fairly polite, put a tick under the +1 column on the Polite–Rude scale. If you think you are extremely impolite, put your tick under the −3 column. If you feel that you are neither specially polite nor specially rude, put the tick under 0 in the middle column.

| | +3 | +2 | +1 | 0 | −1 | −2 | −3 | |
|---|---|---|---|---|---|---|---|---|
| Polite | | | | | | | | Rude |
| Friendly | | | | | | | | Unfriendly |
| Organized | | | | | | | | Disorganized |
| Warm | | | | | | | | Cold |
| Relaxed | | | | | | | | Uptight |
| Open | | | | | | | | Devious |
| Up to date | | | | | | | | Old-fashioned |
| Efficient | | | | | | | | Inefficient |
| Experienced | | | | | | | | Inexperienced |
| **Totals** | | | | | | | | **Totals** |

When you've finished, add up your total score in each column, and then add these together to get a 'total total'. If it comes to a **plus** figure, then you've rated the overall impression you give quite positively. If it comes to a **minus** figure, you need to think hard about what you are writing.

**33**

Few of us could claim that the way we **want** to be perceived, and the way we **actually** present ourselves match up exactly. Why not ask some of the people to whom you send written communications to score you on the 'impressions' scale? It might point to how you could improve your self-presentation.

We will deal with some of these issues later, but if you want to ensure that your written material portrays you as businesslike, competent and efficient, you should consider whether:

- the documents are clearly identifiable;
- they are neatly presented and clearly laid out;
- the key messages are clearly set out;
- the statements are accurate;
- the language is clear and straightforward;
- the grammar and spelling are free from silly errors.

# 5.2  Spelling and grammar

## Activity 22

2 mins

This notice contains various errors of spelling and grammar:

> **The heating controls in this area must not be altared, they are pre-set by the engineers and this can damage them. The settings are done to acheive a proper heating at all times even if cold first thing.**

The meaning of this notice is fairly clear, but what effect would the errors have?

_____

_____

_____

_____

A lot of people who read the notice may not realize there are errors, but you can bet your life that someone will. And that someone is going to think less of the writer as a result. In other words, the writer's credibility will suffer.

I am not going to explain everything that is wrong with the notice in our example, but here is an improved version of it:

> **The heating controls in this area are pre-set by the engineers to provide the correct level of heating throughout the day. Even if it seems cold first thing, please do not alter the settings, as this can cause damage.**

Correct spelling means learning words as you go along. No-one can claim to spell everything perfectly, because there are so many long and complicated words in the language. But it is very embarrassing to have your spelling corrected, and it is well worth trying to improve your spelling skills.

# Activity 23

6 mins

You will need a dictionary for this Activity, which is about checking your spelling. Tick the words that are correct, and write down the correct spelling of those that are wrong:

|  | |  |
|------|---|-----------|
| Tabulation | ☐ | _____ |
| Committee | ☐ | _____ |
| Fulfill | ☐ | _____ |
| Necessary | ☐ | _____ |
| Preparation | ☐ | _____ |
| Perceive | ☐ | _____ |
| Bussiness | ☐ | _____ |
| Arguement | ☐ | _____ |
| Queue | ☐ | _____ |
| Solusion | ☐ | _____ |
| Corparation | ☐ | _____ |
| Defendant | ☐ | _____ |
| Coranory | ☐ | _____ |
| Instalment | ☐ | _____ |
| Segment | ☐ | _____ |
| Independent | ☐ | _____ |
| Discipline | ☐ | _____ |
| Greavance | ☐ | _____ |
| Promise | ☐ | _____ |
| Equipped | ☐ | _____ |

**EXTENSION 2**
Several straightforward but comprehensive guides to grammar are available. They are non-academic, and give you plenty of examples and opportunities to practice. My choice is *The Heinemann English Grammar: An Intermediate Reference and Practice Book*, but in a large bookshop you may find other versions that you prefer. In the meantime, when you are sending out important letters on which a lot depends, get someone more experienced to check your final draft!

I hope you found that dictionary Activity useful – obviously I don't need to give you the correct answers.

It's a good idea to keep a dictionary handy whenever you have to write something. It only takes a few moments to check how to spell a word you are unsure about, and guessing wrongly can cause a lot of embarrassment! There are a number of good-sized pocket dictionaries on the market. Why not invest in one? And while it is no substitute for improving your spelling, if you use a computer word-processing program, its spell-checker function can help you avoid silly errors.

Grammar is a less clear-cut issue than spelling: it means the rules on how we should put our words together. This is an example of bad grammar:

'Where's them memos what I wrote this morning?'

Although many people would indeed say something like that, most listeners would agree that it was incorrect grammar, which always seems worse when it is written down. The correct way to put it would be:

'Where are the memos that I wrote this morning?'

Correct grammar is just as important as correct spelling, but it is much too big a subject for us to deal with here. But think about this issue seriously: bad grammar and bad spelling always give a poor impression, no matter how efficient you are in your job.

---

**Portfolio of evidence D1.1**

# Activity 24

1–2 mins

Author's confession: For some reason I keep coming across the word 'heuristic'. Every time I do, I look it up in the dictionary, but I still can't remember what it means. Solution: write the meaning down!

**This Activity may provide the basis of appropriate evidence for your S/NVQ portfolio. If you are intending to take this course of action, it might be better to write your answers on separate sheets of paper.**

The meaning of words, correct spelling, correct grammar and useful phrases are things that we pick up as we go along – often because we've made a mistake and someone has corrected us. This is a lot easier if you keep a notebook to jog your memory, so for this Activity I suggest you try compiling a 'Writer's Handbook' of your own.

There are three ways to do this:

- buy a pocket notebook and divide it into sections;
- use pages from your personal organizer, if you have one;
- set up a database on your desk-top computer, if you use one.

EXTENSION 3
If you are not confident about avoiding common errors in writing, you may find it helpful to look at Extension Three. This is a brief guide to two of the trickier areas: plurals and using apostrophes. If you're never quite sure when to write **its** and when to write **it's**, this extension will help you get it clear.

The headings I suggest are:

- new words and their meanings;
- short alternatives for longer words;
- simple alternatives for longer phrases;
- words you find difficult to spell;
- useful turns of phrase.

Your Writer's Handbook can become a valuable tool that will be useful for years to come. Be sure to keep it handy whenever you write!

## 6 The human touch

Writing simple, clear letters, memos and reports which read well will do a lot to improve our reputation for communicating well but, as we mentioned at the beginning of this part of the workbook, we may still feel that what we write sounds rather cold and impersonal. So how can we get round that problem?

Let's look at a few simple techniques we could use.

## 6.1 People matter more than things

Look at this pair of sentences.

'Every effort will be made.'

'We shall make every effort.'

In the first sentence the emphasis is on the effort. In the second sentence the emphasis is spread between 'we' and 'effort' so we learn from that sentence what is being made ('every effort') and who is making it ('we').

Sometimes, of course, we want to emphasize a thing rather than a person but, as a general rule, if you write in this impersonal way for any length, you create a rather cold, remote effect which doesn't give a very favourable impression.

**37**

## Activity 25

*3 mins*

Here are **two** more sentences written in a similar way to the one we've just looked at. Rewrite each sentence so that the emphasis is on the person as much as on the thing.

Enquiries will be dealt with by Marilyn Smith.

_____

Your application has been received by the Personnel Officer.

_____

I would have completed the sentences as follows.

- Marilyn Smith will deal with enquiries.
- The Personnel Officer has received your application.

Your wording may not be quite the same as mine but I hope it is on the same lines.

Perhaps you can see what I mean about the rather cold, remote effect created by writing that emphasizes things as opposed to people when you read the following.

## Activity 26

*3 mins*

Here are some more examples of rather cold, impersonal writing.

Improve them by using 'I' and 'we' and by changing the wording where you think it is appropriate.

Applications will be dealt with in order of receipt.

_____

_____

The decision will be conveyed to you by my secretary.

_____

_____

**38**

All arrangements will be confirmed by this office.

_____

_____


It is regretfully felt that the company is unable to provide further assistance.

_____

_____


Here is how I would rewrite each of these sentences. Of course, your version may differ slightly from mine.

- We shall deal with applications in the order we receive them.
- My secretary will let you know the decision.
- We shall confirm all arrangements.
- I'm sorry that we're no longer able to help. (Or: I'm sorry that we can't help any further.)

In some situations, it may be reasonable to appear cold and impersonal – for example when replying to a solicitor's letter or a formal complaint of some kind. It has also been traditional to write technical and other reports in a very impersonal style, but even this is changing. Where people used to write things like:

'Clocking-on procedure was observed 14 times.'

we might now write:

'I observed clocking-on procedure 14 times.'

I also think that writing:

'I discussed the proposals fully with the entire workteam and we reached the following conclusions . . .'

is just as clear and efficient, but more human than:

'The proposals were fully discussed with the workteam and the following conclusions were reached . . .'

# 6.2 The personal touch

Finally, we can often make what we write sound more human if we spend a few moments adding a personal touch – even to an everyday memo or business letter.

I don't mean by this that we should write in a gossipy style like this:

**'I observed clocking-on on the nightshift 14 times. Jolly cold it was too! Still, here are the results anyway.'**

Organizations don't communicate – people do. Yet in the letter we looked at in Activity 17 on page 27, the writer is pretending to be an organization. This is why the letter comes across as so formal, cold and impersonal. This is achieved partly by using bureaucratic language, but the writer uses three other tricks:

- beginning the letter 'Dear Sir' instead of using the person's actual name;
- writing 'we' instead of 'I';
- using 'passive' forms ('your order has been expedited') instead of active ones ('we have expedited . . .'). We'll say a bit more about this later.

The personal touch in business correspondence was once completely forbidden, but times have changed. Most people now feel that writing 'I', addressing people by name, and even using abbreviations (such as 'don't' and 'couldn't') helps get better results because it establishes a more human relationship between sender and receiver. However this does still depend on the context; for example, a hospital administrator replying to a complaint about treatment would be wise to retain a more formal tone.

> Use the right 'sign-off' for your letters: 'Yours faithfully' is on the impersonal side (it's normal to use it in letters that begin 'Dear Sir/Dear Madam'); 'Yours sincerely' is more personal, and should be used when you address someone by name. 'Yours truly' is very personal – keep it for people you're personally friendly with.

## Activity 27

6 mins

Rewrite the letter on page 27, making it simpler, plainer and more human. The customer's name is Nazreem Khan, and the order number was NK 0556/03 (dated 11 January 1996).

_____

_____

_____

_____

_____

_____

_____

There are several better ways of putting the letter, but I think this would work quite well:

---

Dear Mr Khan

**Your order no. NK 0556/03 dated 11 January 1996**

I apologise for the late delivery of your order for 24 HP 8MB SIMM cards.

We have now despatched the cards, and they should reach you by 31 January. Please give me a call if there is any further problem.

Yours sincerely

---

> It's always worth asking yourself if your memos (and all the copies that sometimes get sent) are really necessary. Scrap a memo and save a tree!

Incidentally, I think I would almost certainly send this letter by fax, rather than post, to make sure the information reached the customer as early as possible.

Sometimes the addition of a single sentence is enough to achieve the desired effect:

- 'Thank you for your letter of . . .'
- 'Thank you for your support.'
- 'I look forward to seeing you at the next meeting on . . .'
- 'Please let me know if I can be . . .'
- 'If you need any further help please . . .'.

Any of these may be suitable to assure whoever you are writing to that you are human and that you realize they are too.

And, once you get into the habit of including a comment like these, it becomes an almost automatic response and not something over which you have to chew your pen for hours!

You might find it useful to answer the following Self-assessment questions now before we go on to look at getting our ideas organized when we write.

# Self-assessment 2

15 mins

1 Here is string of long-winded expressions. Try to come up with **one**, or perhaps **two**, words which could replace them.

a Establish a connection between _____

b Pay due attention to _____

c In the vicinity of _____

d Reach a consensus _____

e Under no circumstances whatsoever _____

f At every available opportunity _____

g Without the slightest reservation _____

h Arrive at the conclusion _____

i Reach the decision _____

j It may well be that _____

k With a fair degree of probability _____

l Unable to proceed further _____

m In addition _____

n Poorly illuminated _____

o Socially withdrawn and inhibited _____

p At the present moment in time _____

q Render assistance to _____

r Provide the necessary resources _____

s On a subsequent occasion _____

t Ascertain the location of _____

2 Fill in the missing elements from this diagram of the communication process:

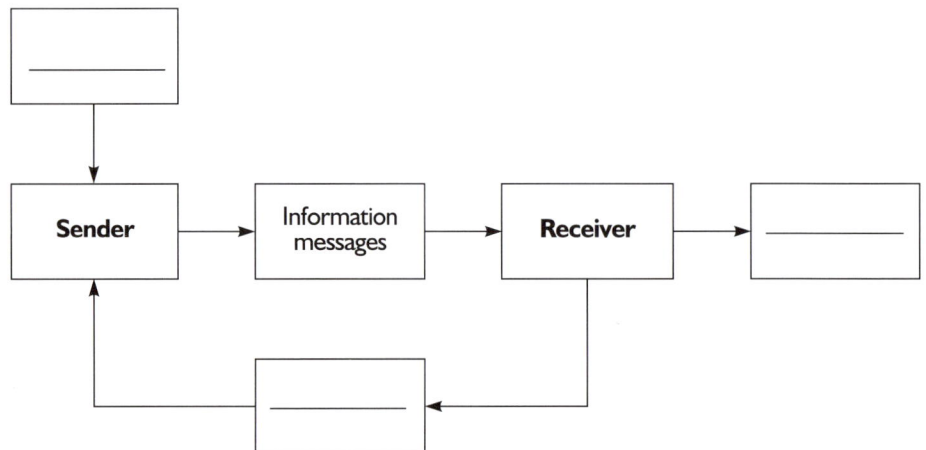

3 Rewrite the following paragraph so that the writer is not 'hiding behind' the company:

'The company does not normally deal directly with the public, and it is usually recommended that you contact the retailer first. However, since the problem is urgent, a replacement unit will be sent to you direct from this office.'

_____

_____

_____

_____

_____

4 Highlight the correct words to use in this sentence, from the choice offered (use a dictionary to check the meanings if in doubt):

'You have my (assurance/insurance/ensurance) that I will do everything necessary to (assure/insure/ensure) that the life (assured/insured/ensured) on your policy is that of your husband.'

5 Here's an anagram: can you rearrange the letters to make a useful four-word slogan for writers?

DOE KITTEN LEAPS SHRIMP

_____

6 Here are **four** sentences containing grammatical errors. Rewrite them correctly.

a Lettuce's 69p each.

_____

b The government has made a serious mistake in their calculations.

_____

c The team won't have nothing to do with a suggestion of that sort.

_____

d Where's the memos that I wrote?

_____

7 Rewrite these **five** sentences to make them more direct and 'human'.

a The Mayor will be greeted by the Managing Director.

_____

b Improvements will have been made by that time.

_____

**43**

c  Responsibility may have to be taken by myself.

_____

d  It was overlooked.

_____

e  Normal practice is to reply in writing.

_____

8  How may words did we save by rewriting the sentences in question 7 in a more direct form?

_____

Answers to these questions can be found on page 95.

# 7 Summary

- The first priority in written communication is to ensure that the messages actually reach their destination. Check fax numbers and addresses and if necessary check that the document has arrived.

- It pays to make the reader's task as simple as possible:

  - identify the writer, target, purpose and content clearly
  - make it easy to read by:

    - keeping it short;
    - using plain and simple language;
    - making the key messages clearly visible;
    - laying the document out so that it's easy to read.

- Accuracy, brevity and clarity are a must for all written communications.

- It's a bad idea to use too many long words:

  - it makes your material more difficult to understand
  - it may give a wrong impression of you as a person
  - both you and the reader may misunderstand some words.

- In the English language there are many alternative ways of saying practically everything. On the whole the shorter ways are better: they will help your messages get through more easily.

- The flowery old-fashioned language that used to be normal in 'business correspondence' has little place today, though some organizations prefer more formality than others.

- On the whole, you communicate better when you use direct forms of writing and show the reader that you are a human being, and do not pretend to be a machine or an organization.

- The written communications may be one of the factors by which quality is judged in an organization.

- Your writing style, spelling and grammar will, whether you like it or not, give your readers a particular impression of you. Make sure you are giving the impression you want to give.

- To make your writing sound human you should:

  - emphasize the people in your sentences rather than the things (i.e. write actively rather than passively);
  - use 'I' and 'we' rather than writing impersonally (with the possible exception of technical reports);
  - try to include a personal touch – a recognition of the reader's involvement – when writing memos and letters.

# Session C Organizing and presenting your ideas

## 1 Introduction

Millions of words are written every day, and your messages are going to have to compete with them. You therefore need to make the reader's task as easy as possible. We have considered some ways of making your words and phrases clearer and simpler. Now we need to think about structure and the visual appearance of the document.

In Session B we talked about standard forms for letters, memos, faxes and e-mails. I explained that one reason for using them was so that the receiver could instantly see what and who were involved. In other words, a clear structure made reading and understanding easier.

When we're talking about slightly longer letters, memos, short reports, factsheets etc., there are a lot more words to read, and the benefits of a clear and logical structure are even greater. The workbook on *Projects and Report Writing* goes into this in more detail, but the same ideas can be used even in quite short bits of writing.

## 2 Tips for organizing written documents

### 2.1 Use headings

Skim through any part of this workbook, and you will see that it is organized under headings. These come in several levels, for example:

Session B  Writing for results

3 Getting the reader's attention

3.1 Keeping it short and simple

Headings are a way of grouping ideas. We could also show similar structures as diagrams, as the case study below shows.

■ Danuta was responsible for preparing the college's information booklet for new students. This involved trying to explain what courses were on offer, and which departments delivered them. She also wanted to name the key individuals heading up the departments. It was perfectly possible to do this in text form, as a series of lists, but the result was very dull and didn't really show how the departments related to one another. She opted for a diagram:

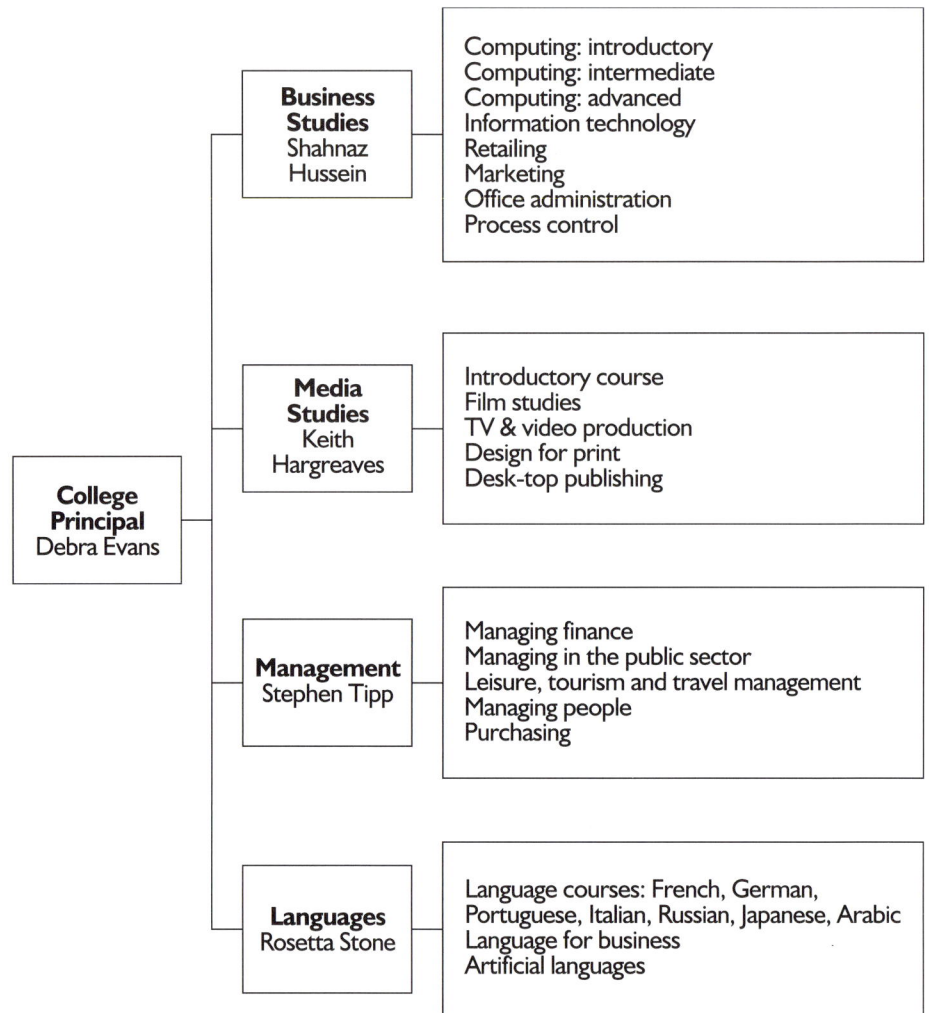

| **College Principal** Debra Evans | | |
|---|---|---|
| | **Business Studies** Shahnaz Hussein | Computing: introductory<br>Computing: intermediate<br>Computing: advanced<br>Information technology<br>Retailing<br>Marketing<br>Office administration<br>Process control |
| | **Media Studies** Keith Hargreaves | Introductory course<br>Film studies<br>TV & video production<br>Design for print<br>Desk-top publishing |
| | **Management** Stephen Tipp | Managing finance<br>Managing in the public sector<br>Leisure, tourism and travel management<br>Managing people<br>Purchasing |
| | **Languages** Rosetta Stone | Language courses: French, German, Portuguese, Italian, Russian, Japanese, Arabic<br>Language for business<br>Artificial languages |

# 2.2 Use numbering

Headings show which points logically go together. Numbering makes this even clearer. It also helps when you're going to discuss the document with someone, especially over the phone. It's quicker and easier to say 'In section 3.5 you mention that . . .' rather than 'When you discuss mechanization you mention that . . .'. 'Mechanization' could appear anywhere in the document and time is lost while everybody leafs through it to find the right item.

Readers will find that numbered headings and subheadings help when making notes, for the same reason.

You notice that I've used a decimal numbering system. This is simpler and more consistent than something like 1a, 1b, 2a, 2b, etc., where it's possible, in a fairly lengthy document, to become confused about which letter belongs with which number. With a decimal system, each number (1.3, 23.4 or whatever) will appear only once, and will relate to only one subsection.

One point to remember with a decimal system is that it's only the figures after the decimal point which change in any one section. So after 1.9, you continue 1.10, 1.11, 1.12 – not 1.9, 2.0, 2.1.

# 2.3  Use indents

You should usually indent your text so that it matches the level of importance of the subheadings, like this:

---

**Claiming travel expenses**

The arrangements for claiming travel expenses as laid down in the Company Staff Manual are as follows:

1 All staff are entitled to claim expenses for activities where travel is involved, provided that:

   1.1 the duties are duly authorized
   1.2 they take place:
      – during work hours
      – or outside work hours for the purpose of carrying out authorized duties at some other location
   1.3 the claim is properly submitted on the standard form

2 The method of travel should be the cheapest that is reasonably practical, but:

   2.1 staff members may use their own cars where this is likely to save a significant amount of time compared with using public transport
   2.2 for the sake of economy, staff should travel together where possible

3 The rates per mile for using own car are at present:

   | up to 999cc | 25 pence per mile |
   |---|---|
   | up to 1499cc | 32 pence per mile |
   | up to 2499cc | 39 pence per mile |
   | over 2499cc | 43 pence per mile |

---

# 2.4 Put figures in columns

Because of the way we have been taught to handle figures, we find it easier to compare two or more figures or to relate them to each other if they are shown to us vertically rather than presented in the middle of a line of words.

So, if you are writing something which involves several figures, try to arrange them in a simple vertical table. So this:

> Last year we made a total of £1 510 000 from the 'brigadier' range, of which £328 000 was sold to North America, and £229 000 was sold to Europe. Most of the rest was accounted for by UK sales, but £51 500 went to the Far East.

can become this:

My advice is to use tables in very small doses. I once produced a book that was 500 pages long — and 350 pages were nothing but tables. That really was a challenge to the reader's attention span.

| Sales totals | 'Brigadier' range sales last year |
|---|---|
| export sales: | |
| N. America | £328 000 |
| Europe | £229 000 |
| Far East | £51 500 |
| domestic sales | £891 500 |
| Total | £1 500 000 |

# Activity 28

15 mins

Read the memo below. Then rewrite it on the blank memo form provided, improving the structure and layout, and making the document shorter and clearer so that the reader can take in the information more easily.

Hints:

- make notes first;
- think about headings and numbering of sections;
- think about indents;
- think about the way you present figures.

| From: | R. Singh, Site General Manager |
| Subject: | Telephone Costs |
| To: | All Section Leaders |
| Date: | 3 November |

I am very concerned about our rapidly increasing telephone costs. For whatever reason, the bill for the last quarter (July–Sept) is over £1800 compared with £1200 this time last year – an increase of over 50 percent.

Bills for the first two quarters this year were approximately £1400 and £1500 respectively, compared with £1120 and £1090, confirming the upward trend. At this rate, we'll have doubled costs in a very short period. We know that fax traffic is increasing (but fax machines can be programmed to transmit overnight whenrates are cheaper).

We expected that our telephone sales drive would increase costs by 10 per cent in this last quater, but against this, charges overall have fallen by 3 per cent. That means the true excess increase is a massive 43% this quarter! We must do something to get this under control.

The higher morning rate no longer applies, but could you please ask all staff in your section to reduce costs wherever possible. You might stress the benefits of preparing for a call before making it so that time spent actually on the telephone is kept to a minimum. It would also help if staff got into the habit of ringing back or leaving a message rather than holding the line if the person they are calling is not immediately available.

Mobiles can be a problem too. Staff are phoning from mobiles when they could be using ordinary phones or call boxes. Also, it's very expensive to call someone else's mobile, such as contractors or sales people in the field.

Some of these may even be personal calls, and this is possibly a difficult topic. We have never previously attempted to prevent staff making or receiving personal calls – in a small firm like ours there has to be some give and take. I would welcome any suggestions as to what could be done about this side of things. In the meantime, please ask staff to keep personal calls to a minimum and to use the pay phone in the snack bar as far as possible.

R.S.

**51**

From:        R. Singh, Site General Manager

Subject:     Telephone Costs

To:          All Section Leaders

Date:        3 November

A more effective way of laying out this memo can be found on page 100.

**52**

The aim with a written communication like this is to make it as easy as possible for readers to understand what the issues are, where the problems lie, and what action is required.

Grouping the key ideas under numbered headings, with text indents and mini-tables where appropriate helps achieve this.

## 3 Using data and statistics

Much of your day-to-day writing will be quite straightforward, but sometimes you will need to include information in the form of numbers – or data, as we usually call them. This may be when you need:

- to prove a point;
- to communicate the numbers themselves;
- to explain something better than words alone can do.

Data can be confusing or boring, and difficult to present. Just think how many times you skip looking at statistics in newspaper reports or other forms of communication. Nevertheless, statistics and numerical data are vital to the running of a business and to understanding what is happening around us.

## Activity 29

2 mins

Note down **three** examples of data or figures you might find at your workplace.

_____

_____

_____

Obviously the data you have included will depend on the type of work you do. Here are just a few examples:

- overtime hours;
- sales figures;
- sickness rates;
- product prices;
- wastage rates;
- bonus payments;
- profit and loss accounts;
- number of accidents.

**53**

As we have to deal with so many figures in our working lives it is easy to miss some, or not take in all the information. Therefore, we need to be good at presenting figures so that people can take in and understand information quickly.

# 3.1 Collecting your data

Numbers are very important in all organizations. For some – like retailers, manufacturers and businesses in the financial sector – numbers are their lifeblood. But all kinds of organization use numbers for measuring how well they are doing: costs, sales, overheads, activity levels, individual perform-ance, progress of training, wastage and the overall financial picture.

In fact, if you try to make a serious point about any such issue without using numbers to back up your case, you will look rather silly.

Here's an example.

■ Robyn wrote a short note to the General Manager:

'All my staff have worked very hard over the last year, and output is greatly increased. The team is successful all round, and everyone has contributed to this. I realize that this year things are tight, but I would like to recommend that my team should receive a performance bonus of 1% of annual salary, on top of any additional increases.'

The General Manager called her in and gave her a 'roasting'. Apart from not considering the firm's general policy on pay, he said, she had given him nothing but personal opinions.

- where was the evidence that the team had worked harder than last year?
- what were the actual increases in output?
- where was the evidence that everyone in the team had contributed equally?
- what did 'successful' mean, and where was the evidence for it?

He also pointed out that Robyn had made no attempt to evaluate the cost of her proposal, or its impact on budgets for the current year and subsequently. He told her to forget the whole thing unless she was able to present a reasoned case, supported by accurate data.

# Activity 30

10 mins

How could Robyn get the data to support her case?

1 Evidence that the team had worked harder:

_____

_____

_____

2 Evidence of increased output:

_____

_____

_____

3 Evidence that everyone had contributed equally:

_____

_____

_____

4 Evidence of 'success':

_____

_____

_____

5 Cost predictions and forecast of effect on budgets:

_____

_____

_____

Organizations have a strong preference for hard facts: they're considered more meaningful, more reliable and more credible — and they have a businesslike 'feel'.

It may be that some of this information was impossible to get, though a well-managed organization should be able to provide the answers.

1 Evidence of working harder could come from:

- total hours worked;
- amount of overtime worked;
- productivity (output per head);
- data about average speed of completing tasks.

**55**

2 Evidence of increased output should be obvious in any production or activity-based organization. Here are some examples from the work of a housing charity:

- total number of enquiries handled;
- number of enquiries handled per head;
- number of 'clients' found accommodation;
- number of information packs distributed;
- number of presentations given to outside bodies;
- amount of time helplines, advice desks etc. open for business.

3 Evidence of individual performance may not always be easy to find. Obvious sources are:

- appraisal records;
- individual output and productivity (where this can easily be measured, e.g. in assembly work, keyboarding, sales, call handling).

4 'Success' may simply mean meeting or exceeding output targets, but it might also be measured by:

- surveys of customer satisfaction;
- reduced error/wastage rates;
- fall in the number of complaints.

5 Cost and budget information should be easiest of all to calculate, though it may mean consulting Personnel and financial specialists. These days, many first level managers are involved in creating budgets, and have specific responsibilities for controlling costs and ensuring output targets are met.

# 3.2 Numbers and statistics

Numbers – data – are of vital importance in every organization. 'Raw' data (the basic figures before they are processed and analysed) are the most reliable evidence of performance. However, the data usually need analysing before they give us clear answers, and that is what statistics is about. Statistics is a series of techniques for telling us what our data really mean, in particular, how things are changing, and when differences are important. Statistical analysis can be extremely complicated – but for most management purposes, it is very simple.

We will look briefly at two practical aspects of statistics:

- using averages;
- using percentages.

# 3.3 Using averages

An average (or 'mean', to give it its technical name) is the total value of a series of data divided by the number of items in the series.

For example, in the course of a month, Bass Radio issues 248 newsflashes, amounting to a total of 139 minutes of airtime. The average time per newsflash is $139 \div 248 = 0.56$ of a minute ($0.56 \times 60 = 33.6$ seconds). This information could be very useful.

- Producers will know roughly what length newsflashes should be.
- It will be obvious when the content of a newsflash needs cutting down.
- Producers know they can fill in more airtime at no extra cost by making newsflashes longer.
- If different newsreaders and/or editors are involved, they can compare the time their newsflashes take with the average. Is anyone too slow, or too long-winded, or too breathless?

## Activity 31

10 mins

Here is a table of data about the sales performance of five branches of a motoring organization:

| Branch | Takings (£00s) | | | | | | Branch total | Branch monthly ave. |
|--------|------|-----|------|------|------|------|--------------|---------------------|
| | Apr. | May | June | July | Aug. | Sept. | | |
| Sutton | 11 | 15 | 2 | 13 | 13 | 14 | ___ | ___ |
| Ilford | 21 | 18 | 18.5 | 22 | 17.5 | 21 | ___ | ___ |
| Rugby | 17 | 16 | 17 | 18 | 15 | 16.5 | ___ | ___ |
| Exminster | 12.5 | 14 | 13.5 | 12 | 10 | 14 | ___ | ___ |
| Perth | 9 | 10 | 11 | 9.5 | 10.5 | 11 | ___ | ___ |
| monthly total | ___ | ___ | ___ | ___ | ___ | ___ | ___ | |
| monthly ave. | ___ | ___ | ___ | ___ | ___ | ___ | | ___ |

Work out the totals and the averages. Remember that there are six items across and five items down.

The answers can be found on page 101.

Did you make any mistakes? If so, make sure you know where you went wrong. Correct your version if necessary.

## Activity 32

3 mins

Think about the data in the table.

1   Jot down **two** uses to which managers might put it:

_____

_____

2   What problems can you identify in the table and the results you have calculated?

_____

_____

3   'The Perth branch is underperforming'. What comment would you make about this statement?

_____

_____

The data could be used in several ways. Obviously they provide a simple record of monthly sales in these five branches over a six-month period. They can also be used to make comparisons – between branches, and between months. Finally, they can be used to make forecasts about future sales (though we won't go into that here).

There is one obvious problem with the data – the Sutton branch's sales for July are only £200. This figure stands out so sharply that I would expect anyone examining the figures to do two things:

■   to check whether the figure is correct;
■   to try to find an explanation.

Probably the branch was closed for most of the month due to renovation, fire damage, or some such accidental event.

Such unusual figures ought to be removed from the calculation of the average, because they distort the picture of how the branch can normally be expected to perform:

■   Sutton branch average sales April–September:

$68 \div 6 = 11.33$

■   Sutton branch average sales April–September excluding June:

$66 \div 5 = 13.40$

**58**

Finally, is the Perth branch underperforming? Well, it has the lowest average monthly sales in the group, but that may not be the whole story. The shop may be smaller, so may the catchment area, the number of staff may be fewer, and so on. To make a useful comparison of performance, we have to get extra information, and make more calculations.

When you use data in your written material you should always examine it closely. If you don't, you risk making mistakes and inviting criticism.

# 3.4  Using percentages

Apart from the four basic functions of arithmetic – adding, subtracting, multiplying and dividing – doing percentages is the most useful maths skill anyone in management could acquire.

Using percentages is a way of expressing something as a fraction of a relevant total multiplied by

$$\frac{100}{1}.$$

The effect of multiplying by

$$\frac{100}{1}$$

is to create figures which are easier to manipulate than fractions and which make comparisons between different sets of data easier.

■  Cheung was looking at the faults levels on two different models. He found that out of 655 DX4–100 desktop PCs sold, 31 had been returned with faults, whereas only 9 Pentium-100 models had been returned, out of the 136 sold. He therefore assumed that the DX4–100s were a bigger problem.

However, when Cheung got out his calculator he discovered that his impressions were wrong. The fault rate for DX4–100 machines was:

$(31 \div 655) \times 100 = 4.7\%$

for the Pentium-100 machines it was:

$(9 \div 131) \times 100 = 6.9\%.$

In other words, the fault rate on the Pentium-100 machines was nearly half as high again. This difference is worked out as follows:

'raw' difference:          $6.9 - 4.7 = 2.2$

percentage difference:    $(2.2 \div 4.7) \times 100 = 46.81\%$

> Percentages are easy to work with if you know what you're doing. If we sold 65 pots of jam yesterday, and the target for tomorrow is 77 pots, what percentage increase would that be – 18 per cent or 16 per cent? Make sure you understand which is correct and why.

**59**

# Activity 33

5 mins

An abattoir processes varying numbers of beef carcasses every day, and reject rates are very important because they affect profitability. Work out on which days the reject rate was (a) lowest and (b) highest by calculating the percentages as shown above. Calculate the averages too.

| Data: | carcasses processed | carcasses rejected | percentage rejected |
|-------|---------------------|--------------------|---------------------|
| Mon | 219 | 26 | ___% |
| Tues | 168 | 21 | ___% |
| Wed | 199 | 25 | ___% |
| Thur | 244 | 33 | ___% |
| Fri | 140 | 11 | ___% |
| Sat | 128 | 14 | ___% |
| Sun | 185 | 28 | ___% |
| Average | ____ | ____ | ___% |

EXTENSION 4
It isn't the job of this workbook to teach you about mathematics and statistics, but they are very important in almost all management contexts. If you would like to learn more about working with numbers, I suggest you take up this extension.

The answers can be found on page 101.

## 4  Presenting things graphically

'Our reporter gave a graphic account of the sights which greeted her when she entered the village. It was, she said, a vision from Hell.'

We use the words 'graphic' and 'graphically' when we mean 'colourful', 'striking', 'dramatic', and 'attention-catching', and that is precisely what graphics in your written materials are supposed to achieve. We think of something that is 'graphic' as a particularly vivid and easily understood way of depicting something. 'Graphic speech' conjures up pictures in our minds, and pictures (visual communication) are a stronger means of communication than spoken or written words or numbers.

## 4.1  A choice of graphic styles

In text, 'graphics' can include:

- photographs;
- diagrams;
- charts and graphs;
- maps;
- 'screens' from computer programs;
- cartoons;
- technical illustrations.

'Visuals' like these help you communicate more effectively, so it makes sense to use them. This is quite easy, especially if you are working with desk-top computers. The latest computers allow us to incorporate all kinds of visual material – even 35mm slides and stills from video recordings – into text documents, to change their size and shape, and to introduce patterns, shading and so on. This can make a big difference to how documents look and how well they communicate.

One of the simplest kinds of graphics is the diagram. Diagrams can show how various people, objects, processes or ideas relate to one another. Look back to page 48 to see an example.

## 4.2  Presenting data graphically

Wherever you need to include data and tables, it's worth considering whether a graphic would get the message across better.

Try out some rough visual representations of data. Squared paper can be handy for this. It provides a basic scale without the need for rulers and a lot of calculation. You can draw up a more accurate version later, if necessary.

The simplest kind of chart is perhaps the **pie-chart**, which is a straightforward way of showing how the total breaks down into its main components, as in this example.

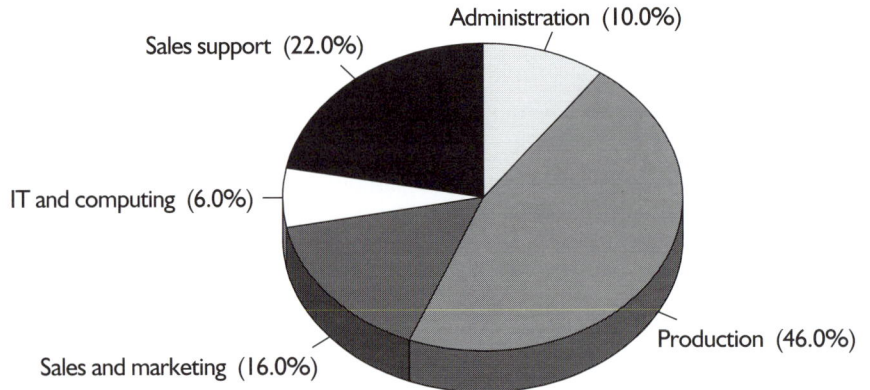

Graphs and bar charts are useful aids to seeing what lies behind the numbers in your tables.

## Activity 34

3 mins

Look at this graph, which plots orders for product **a** and product **b** over a period of months.

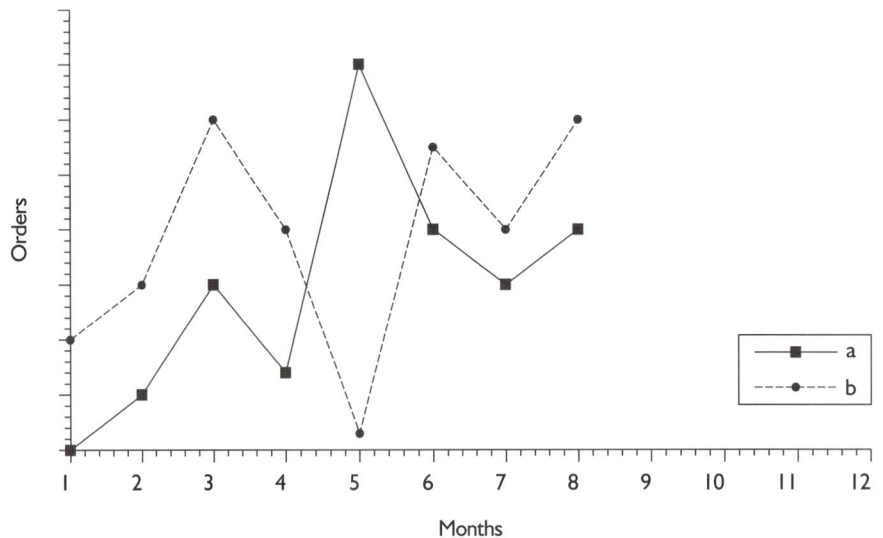

What does it show you?

_____

_____

_____

The graph shows **at a glance** that:

■ orders are on an upward trend;

■ there was a huge fall in orders for product **b** in month 5, and a large rise in orders for product **a**.

The latter cries out for an explanation.

The graph clearly and instantly reveals things that you can only get from tables of figures after a good deal of head-scratching. These are often patterns, as in this example:

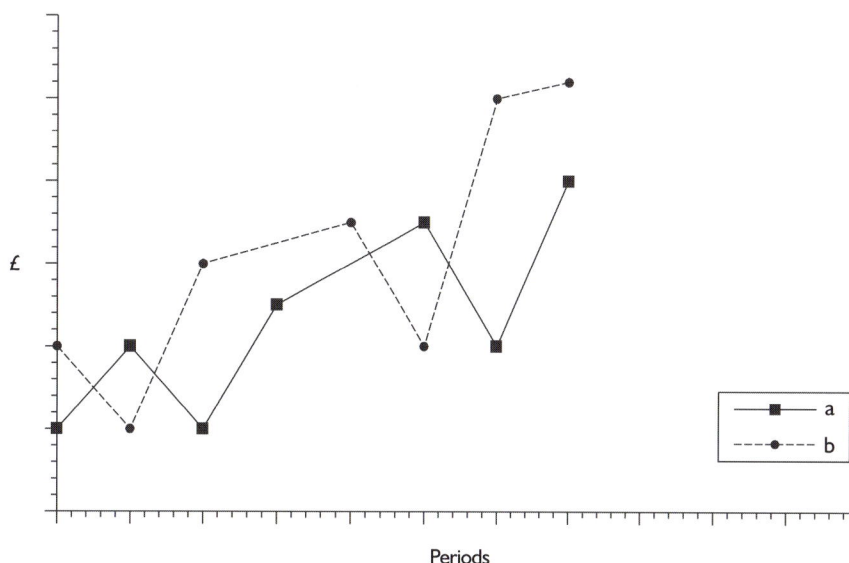

Periods

Here the two lines follow the same pattern, but one is a full period later than the other. Again, this cries out for explanation (perhaps one line is orders received and the other is goods despatched), but the pattern wouldn't have been visible at all in a table.

Patterns, as on this bar chart showing numbers of meals served in a large restaurant, can be very useful for planning.

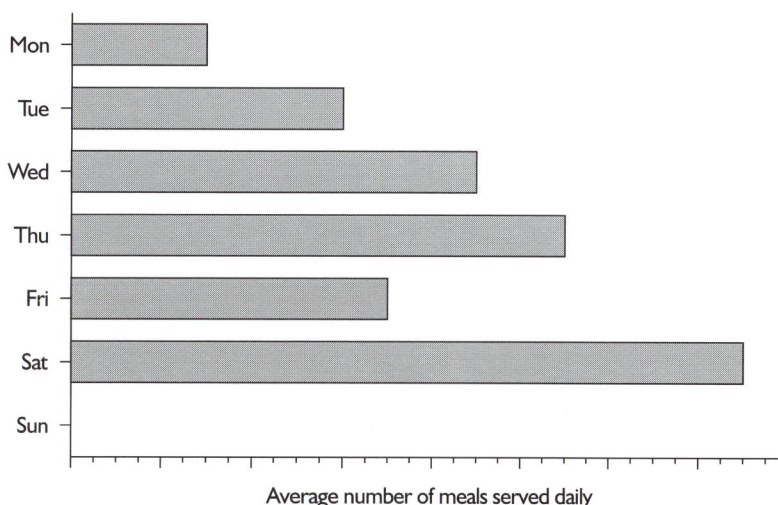

Average number of meals served daily

## Activity 35

⏰ 2 mins

What use would this information be for management and planning purposes?

_____

_____

_____

It tells you clearly when the restaurant is busiest, and therefore when:

■ the largest deliveries of supplies need to be made;
■ how the staffing levels should vary during the week.

# 4.3  Some other kinds of graphics

Newspapers and magazines, whose business is communication, use graphics in all sorts of imaginative ways. For example, magazines like *Which?* use **'matrix' diagrams** to present the results of their tests on consumer products in an easily digestible way.

| Make | Features ratings | | | | |
|------|------|------|------|------|------|
|  | a | b | c | d | e |
| A | ●●● | ●● | ● | ●●●● | ●●● |
| B | ● | ●●● | ●●●●● | ●●● | ●● |
| C | ●● | ● | ●●● | ●●● | ●●● |
| D | ●●●●● | ●● | ● | ●● | ●● |
| E | ●●● | ●●●●● | ●● | ● | ●●●● |

| Features | | |
|------|---|---|
|  | a | ▓▓▓▓▓▓▓▓▓▓▓▓▓▓▓▓▓▓▓▓▓▓▓▓▓▓ |
|  | b | ▓▓▓▓▓▓▓▓▓▓▓▓▓▓▓▓▓▓▓▓▓▓▓▓▓▓▓ |
|  | c | ▓▓▓▓▓▓▓▓▓▓▓▓▓▓▓▓▓▓▓▓▓▓ |
|  | d | ▓▓▓▓▓▓▓▓▓▓▓▓▓▓▓▓▓▓▓▓▓▓▓▓▓ |
|  | e | ▓▓▓▓▓▓▓▓▓▓▓▓▓▓▓▓▓▓▓▓▓▓▓▓ |

Where information has a geographical aspect, you can show it on a map, like this:

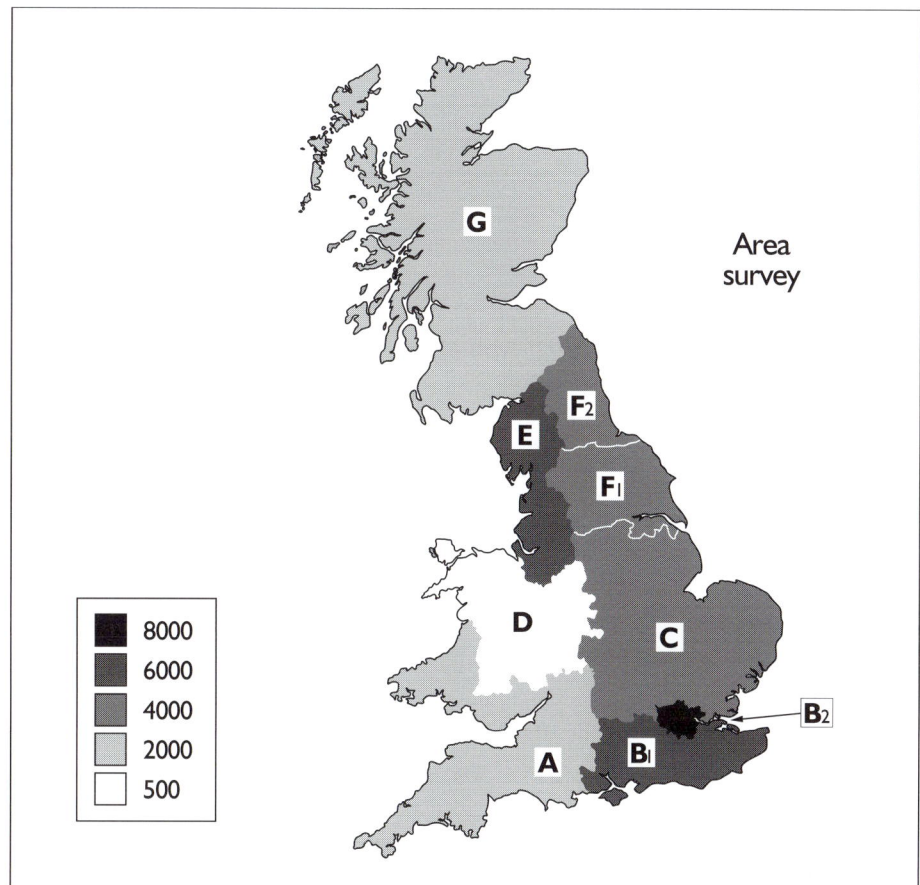

This kind of map can be used to show all sorts of interesting things:

- how spending power varies regionally;
- rates of incidence of various diseases;
- numbers of youngsters in further and higher education;
- pollution rates, car usage, proportion of land in urban use, and so on.

The smallest kind of map is the **floor or site layout plan**. You may also find yourself using these, for example when you are:

- discussing security issues;
- describing an accident;
- explaining some problem of storage, movement or work space.

Unlike graphs and charts, which are easy to create using a computer, and maps, which can be copied from a template of some kind, you may have to draw up layout plans by hand. The key issue is to make them reasonably accurate (this means measuring distances) and by showing the scale.

This has been a very brief introduction to an important subject. For more about the use of graphics, see the workbook on *Project and Report Writing*.

## Self-assessment 3

1 Fill in the blanks to give **three** simple techniques for organizing your written material better:

use _____

use _____

use _____

2 What techniques can you use to draw attention to a particular word, heading or section of your text (hint: look carefully at this Workbook and you should be able to identify at least **four**).

_____

_____

_____

_____

3 Rewrite the following information in the form of a table, to make it legible:

'From 9.00 to 12.00, Alan and Beni will be on duty. Carol will be on from 9.00 to 14.00. Debra will work from 12.00 to 17.00. Alan and Beni come back on at 14.00 after their lunch break and work through till 17.00.'

4 Using a separate piece of paper, turn the table below into a graph.

| Output (units) = No. of surveys booked | | | | | | | | |
|---|---|---|---|---|---|---|---|---|
| Weeks | 1 | 2 | 3 | 4 | 5 | 6 | 7 | 8 |
| London | 15 | 14 | 12 | 9 | 11 | 14 | 15 | 17 |
| Glasgow | 5 | 5 | 4 | 3 | 4 | 4 | 5 | 4 |
| Dublin | 7 | 9 | 12 | 6 | 8 | 9 | 8 | 6 |

5   Define 'average'.

   _____

   _____

6   The company is split between two sites. At Lakeside, there are 321 employees, of whom 248 are part-timers. Of the remainder, only 16 are on Grade F or above.

   At the Forest Way site we have 783 employees, on average, and 344 are part-timers. 260 full-time staff are on Grades C, D and E, and the remainder are on Grade F or above.

   Calculate the following:

   a   the percentage of the total workforce who work at Lakeside

      _____

   b   the percentage of the employees at Lakeside who work full time

      _____

   c   the percentage of the employees at Forest Way who work full time

      _____

   d   the percentage of the total workforce who are on Grade F or above

      _____.

   Answers to these questions can be found on pages 97–8.

# 5 Summary

- To organize your written material better:

  - use headings;
  - use numbering;
  - use indents;
  - put figures in columns to make tables.

- Back up your written documents with data and graphics when you need:

  - to prove your point;
  - to communicate the numbers themselves;
  - to explain something better than words alone can do.

- Make sure you can recognize and calculate averages and percentages from the raw data from your tables.

- Use visual means to communicate numbers and other complex material more effectively:

  - pie charts to show breakdown (or share of various elements within a total);
  - bar-charts to compare quantities and totals;
  - graphs to show how up to four quantities have changed over several periods of time;
  - maps, plans and diagrams to show more complicated relationships.

# Session D  Notes and forms

## 1  Introduction

Most of the writing that we do is designed to communicate to someone else, and this is what the previous sessions have concentrated on. Sometimes, however, we are writing for ourselves, and not for anyone else to see.

The obvious example is a diary – a place where we record our private thoughts and note key dates for the future – but there are several other examples.

■ Yusuf interviewed four candidates who had volunteered to work on the charity's helpline. He asked questions and scribbled rough notes in his notepad as he went along. Looking through his notes the following day he found he had written the words 'Nottingham? – no' against one candidate's name. Try as he might Yusuf could not remember what the note referred to.

Notes can be very important, and it's worth taking more trouble with them.

We will also look briefly at filling in forms and similar routine paperwork. In this case you are certainly writing for someone else (who would fill in those endless routine forms for themselves?!). But while the previous sessions focused on how to structure your own argument, with forms you will need to think instead about what is being requested and how you can respond within the format provided.

■ Renee hated filling in forms – and no wonder! She always started without thinking, had to cross things out, put some entries in the wrong boxes, and used straggly handwriting that took up too much space.

When her handiwork reached its destination, the reaction was often 'What idiot did this?!'

Your paperwork needs to be completed efficiently, or you'll waste your own time and other people's. You also need to think what impression you are giving to the people who read your output.

69

# 2 Personal note-taking

## 2.1 Noting down past events

Managers and supervisors spend a huge amount of their time listening to other people – in meetings, presentations, informal conversations, interviews, and so on. Unfortunately, most of us are not very good either at listening or at remembering.

We find it difficult to concentrate for long periods, especially if we aren't particularly interested in what is being said. And in most cases our memories aren't very long – or very reliable. Considering the huge amounts of information that constantly surround us, this isn't particularly surprising.

It's often said that people only have a very short 'attention span' (the length of time they can concentrate on one thing). Some experts think it's as low as 5–6 minutes. In my experience, most people can concentrate a lot longer than that if they're interested in what's going on!

Of course both memory and concentration work better if we're interested in what's being said: there are plenty of men who can remember all the weekend's football results, but couldn't tell you what they had for dinner!

With practice it's possible to improve memory and concentration, and these are valuable assets for any manager. But the best way to remember what someone has just told you is to write it down. Remember Yusuf in the case study on page 69? He did make notes, but they were only rough. Half an hour after the interview, he could probably have remembered what 'Nottingham? – no' meant; 24 hours later he could not.

In other words, spending a few minutes writing full, clear and legible notes immediately after the conversation, interview, incident (or inspiration, in the case of ideas) will save a lot of wasted effort and frustration later. This example also shows that unless you are a skilled note-taker, making notes is often a two-stage process:

stage 1    make rough notes at the time;
stage 2    go back over them and sort them out.

The rules for notes are:

■  write them now, not later (you may forget);
■  keep them brief;
■  make sure they're clear and legible (so that they will still make sense in a month's time, for instance);
■  organize them logically;
■  have a system for checking that you've acted on them.

# Activity 36

25 mins

**This Activity may provide the basis of appropriate evidence for your S/NVQ portfolio. If you are intending to take this course of action, it might be better to write your answers on separate sheets of paper.**

Here are five different situations in which reliable written notes would have improved efficiency and saved time.

You have two tasks to carry out.

First, what rule would you draw up, based on each situation?

1   **The meeting**

■ Colleen attended a meeting of the safety committee. There were a couple of points about safety in offices that hadn't occurred to her before. She made a mental note to do something about them – but unfortunately she forgot.

_____

**Rule:** _____

_____

2   **The conversation**

■ Kuldeep had a chance meeting with Tessa from sales. Chatting about customer reactions to the new software that Kuldeep's group had developed, she warned him, off the record, of three problems with Version 1.1 that were causing concern. In his own interests, she said, he ought to check them out as soon as possible. When he got back to the office, Kuldeep could remember two of the problems Tessa had mentioned, but the third? … he hadn't the foggiest.

_____

**Rule:** _____

_____

3 Notes of action you have taken

■ Kuldeep called in Sian and Jason. He briefed them on the problems with Version 1.1 and told them to report on (a) what was wrong, (b) how it happened, (c) what could be done about it, (d) how long it would take, and (e) how much it would cost, to get it to him within 48 hours. He carefully noted down what he had asked them, put one copy in his 'action' tray and filed the other for the record.

**Rule:** _____

_____

4 Notes of incidents or actions you have observed

■ Peter was passing through the store's delicatessen area when he saw an assistant rubbing her nose with the back of her hand before picking up and slicing a ham. This was a clear breach of the hygiene rules, but it wasn't Peter's responsibility. When he got back to his office, he carefully wrote down the time and other details, and made a note in his diary to pass it on to the Fresh Foods Manager the following day.

**Rule:** _____

_____

5 Notes of ideas or thoughts you have had

■ During a shift meeting someone mentioned that it was all very well talking about improving the efficiency of the customer enquiry service, but no one knew how long the average call took to answer. It occurred to Rebecca that it might be possible for the on-line accounts software to record this. She made a note to discuss the idea with the other team leaders and get their opinion.

**Rule:** _____

_____

The second stage of this Activity is to collect examples of similar situations that you have experienced personally. You may want to do this gradually over a couple of weeks. For each situation you need to do the following.

a Jot down the date and time of the situation;
b Describe briefly what happened;
c State what notes you made;
d Explain how you used them afterwards.

I think the rules that come out of the five situations are probably these:

1   Always take some notepaper to meetings; jot down important points as you go along.

2   It's less embarrassing to write down points as people make them, than to go back to them later and ask them to tell you all over again.

3   When you give other people detailed instructions, notes will help you follow them up efficiently.

4   Write your notes while the events are still fresh in your memory.

5   Ideas are fleeting things: write them down when they happen, or you'll probably lose them forever.

# Activity 37

*3 mins*

Notes made on the spur of the moment are often handwritten. What are the disadvantages of this, and what could you do about it?

_____

_____

_____

_____

It's really the problem that Yusuf had after his interviews. Rough scribbled notes on the margins of a sheet of paper or on a 'sticky note' are not only difficult for anyone else to decipher (which may or may not be a good thing). They may even be hard for the writer to make sense of, especially when the events or ideas are no longer fresh in the mind.

Also, such notes are scarcely ever complete, and they tend to be 'all over the place', and in the wrong order. Also, when we're making notes of conversations, interviews and so on, we're usually under pressure, so the writing gets more untidy, we miss out whole phrases, words are left uncompleted ... and so on.

They can be excellent 'memory-joggers' – but only in the very short term. There are two ways to get more out of your notes:

1   practice making better notes;

2   check your notes as soon as possible after the event, and:

a   write them up so that you'll be able to understand them days or weeks later
b   fill in any gaps and add any important points that you missed first time round.

**73**

## 2.2 Notes about reading matter

It's often useful to make notes about material that you are reading: articles, books, brochures, letters, reports, etc.

■ Corinne received a copy of a ten-page consultants' report about customer care standards in the business. She was asked to submit comments and proposals on how her own section could improve its performance.

She tackled the report systematically. First she read it straight through quite quickly, to get the general drift. Then she re-read it more carefully:

- highlighting words or passages that she thought were important;
- 'sidelining' and writing '?' against anything she didn't understand;
- writing a few words in the margin where there was an issue she wanted to deal with in her own proposals.

Finally, she went back over her notes and marks, and used them to make more detailed notes as the basis for her response.

---

This approach can be useful in many situations. For example, you may want to:

■ summarize a letter or document so that you can file it away and yet keep the key points in front of you;
■ pass on such information verbally to colleagues or your team;
■ check the minutes of a meeting to see what action you've been committed to;
■ report on a new product or process, based on manufacturer's brochures, technical data sheets and so on.

All these situations call for notes.

Don't be afraid to make notes and highlight passages in books, reports and other documents. It will help you make more sense of them. But don't do it to library books or other people's prized possessions.

> Make notes on your workbook too — NEBS Management Workbooks are deliberately designed with wide margins so that you can do so.

## 2.3 Organizing your notes

I've made the point several times that rough and disorganized notes can be worse than useless. You spend time making them, and then you have to spend even more time working out what they mean, double-checking etc.

Notes, like any other written material, work a lot better when they're properly organized. This means breaking the information down into logical chunks, and skating over unnecessary detail. Suppose you had to report briefly on the potential of the 'voicemail' telephone answering services that are now available. You have to wade through quite a lot of technical and operational information from the supplier, but basically you should concentrate on a short list of key issues:

1   what voicemail is;
2   what it can do;
3   installation and running costs;
4   advantages for cost and efficiency;
5   arrangements for installation;
6   action required (including training staff, informing customers etc.)

Like the more formal kinds of written documents dealt with in Session C, notes need headings, and often (though not always) numbering, too.

---

**Portfolio of evidence D1.2**

# Activity 38

15 mins

**This Activity may provide the basis of appropriate evidence for your S/NVQ portfolio. If you are intending to take this course of action, it might be better to write your answers on separate sheets of paper.**

Practice making notes on a range of documents as if you were going to carry out a team briefing (this is something that you will soon get very quick at doing).

The idea is to develop the ability to read documents and pick out the key points at speed.

The kinds of documents that I have in mind include:

- an internal report (which might be a 'management report' based on analysis of sales and cost data, or a more specialized written report);
- a magazine article relevant to your work;
- a product or technical information brochure;
- minutes of a meeting;
- an external consultant's report.

If your work doesn't bring you such things, then magazine and newspaper articles are a reasonable alternative: libraries contain plenty of suitable material.

It's best to make your notes in three stages:

- first jot down the key messages in the document (you can do this by highlighting them, if you prefer);
- then think about how you will introduce your briefing (e.g. saying where the information came from, and why it's relevant);
- finally note down anything extra you want to say about the key points.

Whether or not you actually carry out a briefing, you will have a quick and thorough summary of the document. This may have many other uses in the future.

## 2.4 Using your notes

**EXTENSION 5**
To find out more about how to make and use notes, especially about your reading matter and so on, you may like to dip into *Effective Learning for Effective Management* by Glenna Sutcliffe. The author has lots of useful hints on note-taking, and explains some handy techniques that we haven't had time to go into here.

I have a very bad habit: I often take notes at meetings, but I scarcely ever look at them afterwards. This is **not** the way to go about it. When you are putting time and effort into making notes, you ought to put them to good use:

■ many notes can be filed (but remember to add the date and a brief description of the circumstances);
■ urgent notes can be pinned up somewhere visible;
■ notes about things you need to do over the next few days can go in your 'in-tray', 'action pile' or whatever.

Your briefcase isn't the best place for 'action notes' – it's too easy to put them inside the wrong folder, or mix them up with other kinds of documents, or simply to forget them altogether.

## 3  Forms and paperwork

Most notes are handwritten (though I recently attended one meeting where a senior person keyed all his notes directly into a lap-top computer – the steady clicking of the keys was quite distracting) and handwriting can be a problem.

Handwriting is also an issue when completing forms – and a lot of jobs involve a lot of form-filling.

It's easy to make a mess of form-filling:

■ writing in the wrong boxes;
■ starting your writing too big and then running out of space;
■ making mistakes and crossing them out;
■ writing untidily.

# Activity 39

5 mins

I think that half the trouble with forms is that people leap in too quickly and start writing without thinking.

Can you suggest a few simple rules for better form-filling? I think there are probably three main ones.

_____

_____

_____

_____

_____

_____

_____

My suggestions are these:

■ look before you write: read through the form to make sure you understand what you're being asked to do;
■ think before you write: work out what you're going to say, and check it will fit in the space provided;
■ write neatly and clearly.

Forms are often badly designed and don't have enough room for all the information they're asking you to provide. So another rule could be:

■ if you need to 'over-run', make this clear on the form and continue (neatly) on a separate sheet; make sure the reader will understand what you have done.

And in general I would advise you to think about your handwriting. Being able to write tidily and legibly is always an asset. Quite simply, it helps you communicate better – and also gives a better impression to others.

# Self-assessment 4

5 mins

1    What's the best way to remember a conversation you've just had?

     _____

2    Decipher this anagram to complete a simple but valuable rule about note-taking:

     TROWEL NO ANT

     Write them _____, _____ _____.

3    Rearrange these words to make the **two** key stages of note-taking:

     stage 1    at make notes rough the time

     _____

     stage 2    and back go out over sort them them

     _____

4    Forms often don't contain enough space for all you need to say. When this happens, what should you do?

     _____

5    When you're filling in forms, what are the **two** things you should do before you start to write?

     _____ and _____.

Answers to these questions can be found on page 98.

# 4 Summary

- We might make notes for one of two main reasons:

  - to remind ourselves about something that happened in the past;
  - to remind ourselves about something we need to do in the future.

- The rules for notes are:

  - write them now, not later;
  - keep them brief;
  - make sure they're clear and legible;
  - organize them logically;
  - have a system for checking that you've acted on them.

- Get more out of your notes by:

  - practising making better notes;
  - checking and rewriting them as soon as possible after the event.

- When preparing notes for a briefing or a short document it's best to make your notes in three stages:

  - first jot down or highlight the key messages in the document;
  - think about how you will introduce your briefing;
  - note down anything extra you want to say.

- Think about your handwriting: it needs to be neat, clear and legible. If it isn't, you will fail to communicate and fail to impress.

- When filling in forms:

  - look before you write;
  - think before you write;
  - write neatly and clearly.

# Performance checks

Write down the answers to the following questions on *Writing Effectively*.

**Question 1**  In general speech has **three** advantages over writing. What are they?

_____

_____

_____

**Question 2**  A written statement creates a permanent record and it is more likely to be accurate than anyone's memory. What is its other big advantage?

_____

**Question 3**  Even if a meeting is minuted, it pays to make your own notes. Why?

_____

_____

**Question 4**  Fill in the blanks so that this passage makes sense:

Speech is fine for getting immediate action and communicating _____ amounts of _____, but it is very ineffective when:

■ the speaker tries to _____ too much _____;

■ the _____ have to _____ it for too long.

**Question 5**  Sometimes we put things in writing because the law requires it. There is another good reason for putting things in writing in situations where the law may in due course be involved. What is it?

_____

_____

**Question 6**  You have an important document that needs to reach a bank in Frankfurt, Germany, within 48 hours. The document is not particularly confidential. You have all normal business communication facilities at your disposal. Describe how you would send the document and ensure its safe arrival.

_____

_____

_____

**81**

Question 7    When busy people receive a written document, what are the first **two** things they need to be able to do?

_____

_____

Question 8    What is the ABC of effective written communication?

_____

_____

_____

Question 9    Translate the following phrases into plain and simple language.

■ enhanced strategies for revenue generation may exist;

_____

■ significantly advantageous consequences may be anticipated;

_____

■ the product has encountered negative consumer reactions

_____

Question 10   This sentence contains minor errors. Highlight them and write the correct version below.

'The principle objection to seperating mens and women's events is that its likely to mean having less paying visiters.'

_____

_____

_____

Question 11   Rewrite the following in a more human and direct way:

'Colleagues' opinions and those of the workteam were sought.'

_____

_____

Question 12   One main advantage of numbering headings in written documents is that it helps the writer organize the material. What is the other?

_____

_____

_____

Question 13    In the seven weeks after a fight broke out during a Council meeting, the local paper received, respectively, 133, 51, 48, 25, 12, 7 and 4 letters on the subject. What is the average number over those seven weeks?

_____

What can we learn from knowing the average?

_____

_____

Question 14    When you make notes about meetings, interviews, conversations etc., it's useful to do this in **two** stages. What are they?

stage 1    _____

stage 2    _____

Question 15    There are **two** basic rules for filling in forms. (Fill in the blanks to complete them.)

■    _____ before you write;

■    _____ before you _____ .

Answers to these questions can be found on page 102.

## 2 Workbook assessment

60 mins

Read the following two letters and then deal with the task which follows, writing your answer on a separate sheet of paper.

The first letter is from a prospective customer, the owner of a hotel in Yorkshire who wants to plant the grounds of the hotel with roses and who is asking for details of what rose trees are available.

The second is from the Customer Service supervisor of A. Savage & Son, specialist rose growers, As you see, the letter from A. Savage & Son contains some useful information but it isn't very well expressed, or logically arranged, or well presented, so that the customer can quickly grasp what he is being told.

Rewrite the letter from A. Savage & Son, using the same information to answer the customer's enquiry but expressing it more simply, logically and helpfully.

You will need to think about:

■    the words and phrases used;
■    the style;
■    the grouping of the main points included;
■    the overall structure.

**83**

# HAWKGARTH HOTEL

Exelby, North Yorkshire

A. Savage & Son                                                      4 August 1996
Reading Road
Binchester
Berkshire
BC2 6QX

Dear Sir

I read with interest the article 'Roses for all reasons' in the Sunday Mail yesterday in which you were mentioned as providing a free advisory service on planting and cultivating roses.

This hotel stands in two acres of grounds which used to be well known in the area for its splendid display of roses. We have several interesting photographs taken before the Second World War which bear this out. However, its requisition during the war as a military establishment, subsequent years of neglect followed by fifteen years use as a boarding school means that the former rose gardens have virtually disappeared.

I anticipate that re-stocking the grounds will take about five years and thought in terms of starting this year with hedges, roses amongst the trees in the woodland and climbers in difficult positions which will all take some years to achieve maturity.

I should be interested to know what you would suggest for the following:

1. Climbers for a north facing, random stone wall of the main wing of the hotel, approximately 80 feet long;

2. A vigorous tall hedge to screen adjoining farm buildings and to deter animals from the farm from coming through the fence onto our property;

3. Ramblers to grow amongst trees on the edge of an existing copse of trees (rather neglected at the moment) in a shaded corner of the grounds. I hoped that planting some roses there would give colour and interest to an otherwise dull area.

I look forward to hearing from you.

Yours faithfully

S. Hamlin

**A. Savage & Son**
Rose Specialist
Reading Road
BINCHESTER
Berkshire
BC2 6QX

Mr S. Hamlin                                                                                    7 August 1996
Hawkgarth Hotel
EXELBY
North Yorkshire

Dear Sir

With reference to your letter of 4 August, we shall be delighted to help you re-stock your rose garden and offer the following suggestions. A copy of our catalogue is enclosed so that you can consider the entire stock list for yourself. The ideal planting time for roses is November/December, though any time until March is possible provided there is no danger of severe frost. However, I do advise you to place your order as soon as possible so that the roses are despatched in time for autumn planting provided, of course, that you are ready to plant them then. Our roses are packed in peat and polythene and will tolerate being kept in dark, frost-free conditions for up to three weeks prior to planting.

As I said, you may like to choose alternatives from the complete stock list but I suggest the following. Alberic Barbier would do well climbing against a north wall and will also grow into trees satisfactorily, though you would have to be careful that roses were not planted too close to the roots of trees and, of course, no roses will do well in totally shaded conditions. However, I think you would find that the following would achieve the effect you want in adding interest and colour to the copse:

Alberic Barbier;
Dr van Fleet;
Bobbie James;
Pauls Himalayan Must;
Wedding Day.

This would give you a variety of colour and flowering periods and the additional interest of coloured hips in the autumn.

In addition to Alberic Barbier as a climber for a north wall, you might like to try Gloire de Dijon, Golden Showers, May Queen and New Dawn. This will also give you a variety of colour. You are fortunate in having random stone walls against which almost every colour is seen to advantage as opposed to brick, for instance, which never does justice to reds and crimsons. However, against a north facing wall, with limited direct sunlight, I think you will find that lighter yellows, pinks and whites create a more pleasing effect. Incidentally, May Queen also makes a splendid tree. As for the hedge, I suggest Nevada, Constance Spry and Fruhlings Gold to give you a variety of colour, though, of course, if you feel that one colour would create a more dramatic effect then you could create a hedge of any one of these. Certainly any of them will give you a tall, impenetrable hedge within a few years.

Judging by the indication of size you have given, I estimate that you would need twelve climbers and fifteen to twenty roses to grow into the copse. You don't give an indication of the length of hedge you require but, to provide a dense hedge of this type you could estimate planting one bush every four feet.

Climbers and the roses for the copse are £3.75 each, hedging plants are £2.75 and we give a discount of 10 per cent on orders over £200. There is a standard charge of £4 per order for packaging and carriage but this is waived on orders over £50.

We can offer a more detailed advisory service than I have given if you provide more detailed information of dimensions, aspect, soil type etc and, if required, we will also come and visit a customer's premises to discuss special requirements though we have to charge for this service. I enclose a questionnaire which you might like to complete and return if you would like more detailed advice on planting your grounds. This service is free.

I wish you every success with your roses and we look forward to receiving your order.

Yours faithfully

R. Harris
Customer Service Supervisor

Enc

# 3  Work-based assignment

60
mins

**The time guide for this assignment gives you an approximate idea of how long it is likely to take you to write up your findings. You will need to spend some additional time gathering information, perhaps talking to colleagues and thinking about the assignment and planning.**

Your work on this assignment may provide the basis of appropriate evidence for your S/NVQ portfolio. If you are intending to take this course of action, it might be better to write your answers on separate sheets of paper.

Choose what seems to you a fairly limited problem at work to which you can think of a solution. This might be:

- a minor change in a clerical system;
- a slightly different way of working;
- a change of material or materials handling;
- a change of storage arrangements;
- something to do with the health, safety or welfare of your workteam.

But those are only suggestions. You may well think of something which doesn't come in any of these categories, and exactly what you choose will depend on the nature of your job.

Perhaps you will think of a problem which you have solved fairly recently. In that case, use it for this project, but assume that your solution hasn't yet been put into operation.

Don't choose anything too ambitious because, as you know, it's rarely simple to bring about a major change in one work area without affecting the work of a lot of other people.

Having chosen your problem and its solutions, write a memo to your immediate boss describing precisely what the problem is and what you suggest to improve the situation. Remember to provide enough evidence to support your case and write it in a way which is likely to get a favourable response.

Next assume that what you propose has been agreed to and you can make the change.

How would you inform your workteam?

Would you need to back up anything you say in writing? In one or two sentences write down what you would do to make sure that your workteam took notice of the change you were making and remembered it whenever necessary.

Finally, write out **one** of the pieces of written information which you might use to get your workteam to make the change you suggest effectively and efficiently. This might be a memo, a notice or notes for a briefing session, but need not necessarily be any of these.

# Reflect and review

## 1  Reflect and review

Now that you have completed your work on *Writing Effectively*, let us review our workbook objectives.

■ When you have completed this workbook you will be better able to decide when it is more useful to write than to speak, and when a combination of the two is even more useful.

In Session A we had a lot to say about the advantages of speech versus the advantages of writing, and pointed out various situations in which writing would be preferable. Emergencies, informal situations and meetings obviously call for speech. But when people are distant, facts need to go on the record, and when more complex ideas are being communicated, writing clearly has the edge.

Now you have completed your reading and responded to the Activities, you should perhaps have a clearer idea of when to write rather than speak. The best way to test this is perhaps to ask about situations where you might use both!

■ In what situations would you opt for writing first, **but back up your messages with speech**, and why?

_____

_____

_____

_____

■ In what situations would you opt for speech first, **but back up your messages in writing**, and why?

_____

_____

_____

_____

The second objective is:

■ When you have completed this workbook you will be able to give your written communications a better chance of:

- reaching their destination;
- being noticed;
- being read;
- being understood.

Many factors are involved in this, but the key is to think about how you can make the reader's job easier. Achieving this involves:

1 administrative matters like clearly addressing and identifying your documents;

2 language skills (mainly the ability to write in a simple and straightforward way);

3 physical issues, especially choosing a clear and attractive layout;

4 the ability to structure your ideas and material logically;

5 good judgement as to where to insert tables and graphics, and the technical ability to create them.

Now's the time to review how much you've achieved in these five key areas. Rate yourself out of ten on each of them, and make a brief note of where you feel your weaknesses and strengths presently lie.

1 Administrative matters     Rating ☐

_____

2 Language skills     Rating ☐

_____

3 Use of layout     Rating ☐

_____

4 Logical structure     Rating ☐

_____

5 Use of tables and graphics     Rating ☐

_____

The final objective is:

■ When you have completed this workbook you will be better able to remind yourself of ideas, messages and events by making clear and legible notes.

College and university students get into the habit of taking notes, because they have to. For most of the rest of us, it is a much more haphazard business. Yet notes can be useful in scores of different situations, and in many they are vital. Human memory simply isn't up to making a faithful record of the vast amount of spoken and written information that is continually pouring towards us. Notes are the only way.

Unfortunately, most of us are very unsystematic about notes. This workbook has, by contrast, tried to show the benefits of being disciplined and consistent with your notes.

■ In what situations are you taking and using notes now, where you were not doing before?

_____

_____

_____

_____

■ What rules do you follow about taking and using notes, for example of meetings, conversations and interviews?

_____

_____

_____

_____

# 2 Action plan

Use this plan to further develop for yourself a course of action you want to take. Make a note in the left-hand column of the issues or problems you want to tackle, and then decide what you intend to do, and make a note in Column 2.

The resources you need might include time, materials, information or money. You may need to negotiate for some of them, but they could be something easily acquired, like half an hour of somebody's time, or a chapter of a book. Put whatever you need in Column 3. No plan means anything without a timescale, so put a realistic target completion date in Column 4.

Finally, describe the outcome you want to achieve as a result of this plan, whether it is for your own benefit or advancement, or a more efficient way of doing things.

| Desired outcomes | 1 Issues | 2 Action | 3 Resources | 4 Target completion | Actual outcomes |
| --- | --- | --- | --- | --- | --- |
| | | | | | |

## 3  Extensions

**Extension 1**

Communication by fax has both advantages and disadvantages.

- Advantages

  - It is much quicker than the post (thus allowing at least a day more for preparation).
  - Handwritten notes can be attached.
  - An accurate copy of the document is delivered.
  - When a fax arrives, it is physically visible, unlike an e-mail message.
  - Even if the intended person doesn't notice it, someone else may (though this can be a disadvantage too).

- Disadvantages

  - Faxes can go astray, and transmission can fail.
  - The potential for 'last minute' transmission encourages us to delay preparing and sending our material until the last minute.
  - The last minute sometimes turns out to be too late.
  - The print quality of faxed documents is often rather poor.
  - Long paper documents can take a long time to send.
  - Faxed documents cannot be substituted for the 'originals' that are often required by the law (in contracts and as legal evidence, for example).
  - There is a lack of privacy/confidentiality.

Computer e-mail, which is the fastest-growing channel for written communications, offers an interesting new option but also has its own serious risks. Many people find it useful for short or urgent messages that might otherwise be delivered via a phone call. Often the style is informal and more like spoken conversation.

Longer documents can be sent by e-mail, often as 'attachments' to be printed out at the other end.

The advantages and disadvantages of e-mail are these:

- Advantages

  - It can be the quickest communication channel (and thus, like faxes, e-mail messages can be left until the last moment).
  - It is handier than paper faxes for sending longer documents that were generated or stored on a computer.
  - The sender can see whether the mail has reached its destination (many organizations have internal e-mail systems that can also tell the sender whether the receiver has 'read', i.e. opened, the document).
  - Internal e-mail systems provide a confidential and private way to send messages for the eyes of the recipient only (when using external links such as the Internet, senders can protect their messages by using passwords or even encryption).

**91**

■ Disadvantages

- E-mail isn't useful at all if the other party doesn't have an e-mail 'address' (people are still more likely to have access to a fax).
- The potential for last-minute transmission can cause the same problems as outlined above for faxes.
- Like faxes, e-mails will not be accepted as 'original documents' for legal purposes.
- Most importantly, the priority given to e-mails may vary with different people. There is no physical piece of paper to land on someone's desk, and the receiver may ignore the 'electronic mailbox' for days on end. This problem is encouraged by the large amount of e-mail traffic which, due to the novelty of the medium, is of a trivial and low-priority nature.

**Extension 2**

Book      *The Heinemann English Grammar: An Intermediate Reference and Practice Book*
Edition    Second edition 1992
Authors   Digby Beaumont and Colin Granger
Publisher  Heinemann

Most of us think of grammar as a very dusty and tedious subject, but it's really about the correct (and accepted) way to express yourself. In ordinary speech correct grammar doesn't always matter. When you are writing, and your writing will be seen by people who **do** know their grammar, it pays to get it right. This book (and several similar publications by other publishers) will help you do that, and if you have any interest in how language works, you'll find it enjoyable too.

**Extension 3**

Many people have difficulty with plurals, and end up getting them wrong. A common mistake is to use an apostrophe-S, as in these examples:

'Lettuce's only 40p.'

'Girl's and boy's wanted for delivering newspaper's.'

For most words, the correct way to form a plural is simply to add S:

| **Singular** | **Plural** |
|---|---|
| ratchet | ratchets |
| programme | programmes |
| warehouse | warehouses |
| inspector | inspectors |
| kitten | kittens |
| colleague | colleagues |
| tree | trees |
| breakfast | breakfasts |
| album | albums |
| limb | limbs |
| pudding | puddings |
| expedition | expeditions |

**Never** use apostrophe-S to make a plural: **limb's** and **programme's** are wrong.

With some words, you make the plural by adding ES:

| Singular | Plural |
|----------|--------|
| watch | watches |
| carcass | carcasses |
| tomato | tomatoes |

Words which end in Y, change to IES:

| Singular | Plural |
|----------|--------|
| city | cities |
| activity | activities |

And there are some very common words which change in different ways:

| Singular | Plural |
|----------|--------|
| woman | women |
| mouse | mice |
| sheaf | sheaves |
| goose | geese |

So when do we use the apostrophe-S?

It **never** indicates a plural. **Either** it is a shortened version of 'is' or 'has', **or** it indicates belonging.

| Short for is or has | Belonging |
|---------------------|-----------|
| The ratchet's broken. | The ratchet's teeth are broken. |
| The summons's on the table. | The summons's wording is wrong. |
| The city's a mess. | So are the city's inhabitants. |

The word that writers most often get wrong is **its/it's**.

**Its** without an apostrophe indicates 'belonging to'; **it's** with an apostrophe is short for **it is** or **it has**. For example:

'Look at that mouse – it's lost its tail!'

**93**

Correct spelling means learning words as you go along. No one can claim to spell everything perfectly, because there are so many long and complicated words in the language. But it is very embarrassing to have your spelling corrected, and it is well worth trying to improve your spelling skills.

**Extension 4**

| | |
|---|---|
| Book | *A First Course in Statistics* |
| Author | D.J. Booth |
| Edition | Second edition 1992 |
| Publisher | DP Publications |

There are plenty of books dealing with basic business numbers and statistics, and this is one of the more straightforward ones. Since it is designed as a course book, it includes coverage of some more advanced and complex subjects that probably won't be relevant to your needs. Nevertheless, you will find a range of useful and work-relevant material here.

**Extension 5**

| | |
|---|---|
| Book | *Effective Learning for Effective Management* |
| Author | Glenna E. Sutcliffe |
| Edition | 1988 |
| Publisher | Prentice Hall |

This book covers lots of relevant and useful topics. The most helpful chapters from our point of view are: 4 Listening; 7 Note Making; and 8 Reading Strategies. There are also useful chapters on 'speed reading', using your time more effectively and memory techniques, but the chapters on writing skills and presentations are not so good.

These extensions can be taken up via your NEBS Management Centre. They will either have them or will arrange that you have access to them. However, it may be more convenient to check out the materials with your personnel or training people at work – they may well give you access. There are other good reasons for approaching your own people; for example, they will become aware of your interest and you can involve them in your development.

# 4 Answers to self-assessment questions

**Self-assessment 1 on page 15**

1 My choice of speech or writing in these seven situations is as follows:

a When a member of your team wants advice about a work problem – speech.

b When a legal issue is involved – writing, though there may occasionally be situations where you choose **not** to put something in writing because for legal reasons you would prefer it not to be available.

c It is an emergency and you need action to be taken immediately – speech.

d You need to communicate the same message to large numbers of people – writing (unless all the people are gathered in one place and you can speak to them simultaneously).

e   You need to send your message across time and space – writing.

f   You need to communicate with people at a different location – either.

g   You want to put forward some proposals for discussion at a committee – both.

2   The statements should read as follows:

a   Writing is the best choice if you need to put your words on RECORD.

b   Communicating in SPEECH can be very ineffective when too much INFORMATION is involved and the listeners have to REMEMBER it for too long.

c   An important advantage of communicating in WRITING is that you can get exactly the SAME message to a large number of people.

3   Here are four situations where it would be useful to note the time, date and other details:

■   you received an important message;
■   a particular problem arose;
■   you had a bright idea;
■   you witnessed an incident of some kind.

You may have thought of others as well.

4   'Fax' is short for 'facsimile transmission'.

5   It pays to think before you speak at meetings that are being minuted, because something unfortunate may go on permanent record.

6   For a full list of advantages and disadvantages of fax and e-mail communication, see EXTENSION ONE.

**Self-assessment 2 on page 42**

1   The expressions could be written more simply like this:

a   Link
b   Note
c   Near
d   Agree
e   Never
f   Whenever
g   Definitely
h   Conclude
i   Decide
j   Probably
k   Likely
l   Stuck
m   Also
n   Dim
o   Shy
p   Now
q   Help
r   Equip
s   Later
t   Find

2   The diagram should read like this:

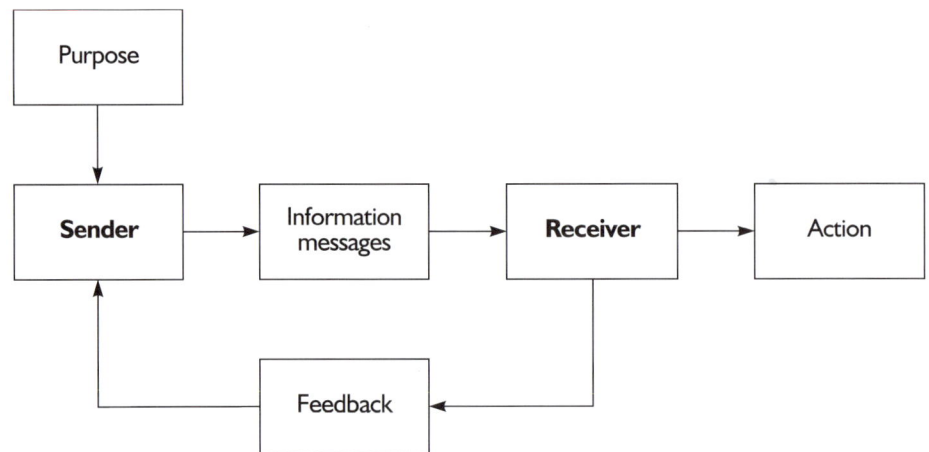

```
          ┌──────────┐
          │ Purpose  │
          └────┬─────┘
               │
               ▼
┌──────────┐  ┌─────────────┐  ┌──────────┐  ┌──────────┐
│  Sender  │─▶│ Information  │─▶│ Receiver │─▶│  Action  │
│          │  │  messages    │  │          │  │          │
└──────────┘  └─────────────┘  └──────────┘  └──────────┘
     ▲                              │
     │         ┌──────────┐         │
     └─────────│ Feedback │◀────────┘
               └──────────┘
```

3   Your wording may differ slightly from mine:

'We do not normally deal directly with the public so I would usually suggest that you contact the retailer first. However, since the problem is urgent, we will send you (or 'I have arranged to send you') a replacement unit direct from this office.'

4   This statement should read:

'You have my ASSURANCE that I will do everything necessary to ENSURE that the life INSURED on your policy is that of your husband.'

5   The anagram, when deciphered, reads: **'Keep it short and simple'**.

6   Here are the four sentences with the grammatical errors corrected. Make sure you can see what I have done.

    a  Lettuces 69p each.
    b  The government has made a serious mistake in its calculations.
    c  The team won't have anything to do with a suggestion of that sort.
    d  Where are the memos that I wrote?

7   You can improve the five sentences like this:

    a  The Managing Director will greet the Mayor.
    b  We will have made improvements by that time.
    c  I may have to take responsibility.
    d  We (or I) overlooked it.
    e  We usually reply in writing.

8   There were 35 words in the original sentences, and 29 in the rewritten version, a saving of 6, or 17.14%.

**Self-assessment 3 on page 66**

1   The three techniques are USING HEADINGS, USING NUMBERING, and USING INDENTS.

2   Techniques you can use to draw attention to a particular word, heading or section of your text include:

- using bold lettering;
- using italic lettering;
- using underlining;
- using larger lettering sizes;
- using 'icons' (small symbols to indicate particular kinds of material);
- using a different colour.

The first four will be available on any word-processing system; the last two require slightly more in the way of skills and equipment.

3   This information can be written down as a simple table like this:

| Hours | 9.00–12.00 | 12.00–14.00 | 14.00–17.00 |
|-------|------------|-------------|-------------|
| Alan  | ✓          | –           | ✓           |
| Beni  | ✓          | –           | ✓           |
| Carol | ✓          | ✓           | –           |
| Debra | –          | ✓           | ✓           |

4

Output (units) – number of surveys booked

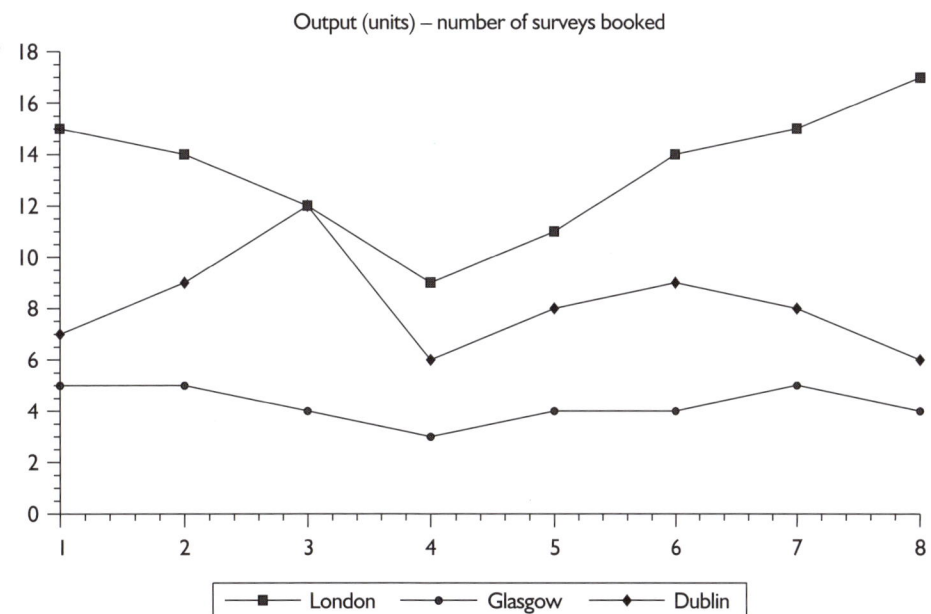

London    Glasgow    Dublin

5   An average (or 'mean', to give it its technical name) is the total value of a series of data divided by the number of items in the series.

6   There are 1104 employees in the company (321 + 783). We have rounded the percentages up to one decimal point.

a   The 321 who work at Lakeside represent 29.1 per cent of the total

(321 ÷ 1104 × 100).

b   The percentage of the employees at Lakeside who work full time is 22.7 per cent

(321 − 248 = 73; 73 ÷ 321 × 100).

c   The percentage of the employees at Forest Way who work full time is 56.1 per cent

(783 − 344 = 439; 439 ÷ 783 × 100).

d   The percentage of the total workforce who are on Grade F or above is 16 at Lakeside plus 783 − (344 + 260) = 179 at Forest Way, a total of 195. This is 17.7 per cent of the total workforce of 1104.

**Self-assessment 4 on page 78**

1   Write the key points down.

2   The anagram 'TROWEL NO ANT' can be deciphered so that the sentence reads:

Write them NOW, NOT LATER.

3   The two stages are:

stage 1   make rough notes at the time;
stage 2   go back over them and sort them out.

4   When forms don't have enough space for all you need to say, the best solution is to write the extra material on a separate sheet, and attach it; you should of course make a note of this on the form itself.

5   When you're filling in forms you should LOOK and THINK before you write.

# 5 Answers to activities

**Activity 16
on page 26**

Which words you would use to replace these long ones depends to some extent on the context, but the ones which occurred to me are:

| Long | Short |
| --- | --- |
| advantageous | useful |
| application | use |
| ascertain | find out |
| commencement | start |
| comprehension | grasp |
| consequently | so |
| deficiency | lack |
| disadvantage | drawback |
| elucidate | explain |
| emphasize | stress |
| excessive | too much |
| expedite | hasten, speed up |
| expenditure | spending |
| facilitate | allow |
| fundamental | basic |
| furthermore | also |
| illustrate | show |
| inventory | stock |
| relationship | link |
| subsequently | later |
| terminate | end |
| unprecedented | new |
| utilization | use |

**Activity 28
on page 50**

I would lay the memo out like this. You may have decided to do it slightly differently.

---

| From: | R. Singh, Site General Manager |
|---|---|
| Subject: | Telephone Costs |
| To: | All Section Leaders |
| Date: | 3 November |

**1 The problem**

Our telephone costs are rapidly increasing – they are over 50 per cent above last year's costs in the last quarter:

|  | last year | this year |
|---|---|---|
| Jan–Mar | £1,120 | £1,400 |
| Apr–June | £1,090 | £1,500 |
| Jul–Sept | £1,200 | £1,800 |

We had forecast an increase of 10 per cent as a result of our telephone sales drive; against this, there has been a 3 per cent reduction in rental and line charges this year. We therefore budgeted for an increase of 7 per cent overall, but this has been greatly exceeded (the net increase is 43 per cent).

**2 Ways of reducing costs**

In order to help bring telephone costs back under control, please encourage all staff in your section to:

2.1  avoid making calls from mobiles;
2.2  avoid making calls to mobiles;
2.3  prepare for calls before making them to keep time actually spent on the telephone to a minimum;
2.4  ring back or leave a message rather than holding on;
2.5  keep personal calls to a minimum (there is a pay phone in the snack bar).

**3 Personal calls**

This may be a difficult issue, as we have never imposed any restrictions in the past. I would be grateful for any suggestions for dealing with it.

R.S.

---

**Activity 31 on page 57**

| Branch | Takings (£00s) | | | | | | Branch total | Branch monthly ave. |
|---|---|---|---|---|---|---|---|---|
| | Apr. | May | June | July | Aug. | Sept. | | |
| Sutton | 11 | 15 | 2 | 13 | 13 | 14 | 68 | 11.33 |
| Ilford | 21 | 18 | 18.5 | 22 | 17.5 | 21 | 118 | 19.67 |
| Rugby | 17 | 16 | 17 | 18 | 15 | 16.5 | 99.5 | 16.58 |
| Exminster | 12.5 | 14 | 13.5 | 12 | 10 | 14 | 76 | 12.67 |
| Perth | 9 | 10 | 11 | 9.5 | 10.5 | 11 | 61 | 10.17 |
| monthly total | 70.5 | 73 | 62 | 74.5 | 66 | 76.5 | 422.5 | – |
| monthly ave. | 14.1 | 14.6 | 12.4 | 14.9 | 13.2 | 15.3 | – | 14.08 |

**Activity 33 on page 60**

| Data: | carcasses processed | carcasses rejected | percentage rejected |
|---|---|---|---|
| Mon | 219 | 26 | 11.87% |
| Tues | 168 | 21 | 12.50% |
| Wed | 199 | 25 | 12.56% |
| Thur | 244 | 33 | 13.52% |
| Fri | 140 | 11 | 7.86% |
| Sat | 128 | 14 | 10.94% |
| Sun | 185 | 28 | 15.14% |
| Average | 183.29 | 22.57 | 12.06% |

My answers clearly show that the lowest rate of rejects was on Friday and the highest was on Sunday. Again there are differences here that would repay closer examination. Why are rejection rates so much lower on Fridays? Was inspection less careful, perhaps? Why was it so much higher on Sunday? Was quality of the cattle received on that day inferior? And why does the rejection rate seem to be rising?

# 6 Answers to the quick quiz

Answer 1    Speech has three advantages over writing:

- speech is more immediate;
- it can have more impact;
- speaking is a lot quicker than writing.

Answer 2    A written statement creates a permanent record and is more likely to be accurate than anyone's memory. Its other big advantage is that it can CROSS BOTH TIME AND SPACE to be used again.

Answer 3    Even if a meeting is minuted, it pays to make your own notes in case later there are disagreements about what was actually said.

Answer 4    This passage should read:

Speech is fine for getting immediate action and communicating SMALL amounts of INFORMATION, but it is very ineffective when:

- the speaker tries to COMMUNICATE too much INFORMATION;
- the LISTENERS have to REMEMBER it for too long.

Answer 5    The other good reason for putting things in writing when the law may in due course be involved is to protect ourselves (it's wise to put down the facts before our memory of them starts to dwindle.)

Answer 6    There are several possible ways of sending (and confirming the arrival of) a document like this within the required timescale:

- the post will not do;
- you could use a courier, but it would be expensive;
- fax or e-mail would both be feasible (and inexpensive) but you would need to make a follow-up telephone call to ensure safe arrival.

Answer 7    When busy people receive a written document, the first two things they need to be able to do are:

- to identify who sent it and what it is about;
- to decide whether it is important or not.

Answer 8    The ABC of effective written communication is ACCURACY, BREVITY and CLARITY.

Answer 9    I would translate the following phrases into plain and simple language as follows:

a   There may be better ways of earning money.
b   We can expect a much better result (or outcome).
c   Customers don't like the product.

Answer 10    This sentence, when corrected, should read as follows:

'The principal objection to separating men's and women's events is that it's likely to mean having fewer paying visitors.'

Answer 11    'We (or I) asked our (or my) colleagues and members of the workteam what they thought.'

Answer 12    The reason for numbering headings in written documents is that it helps the writer organize the material. Its other main advantage is that it helps the reader understand the material more easily (it's also easier to discuss the document when you can refer to sections by number).

Answer 13    The average number of letters is 40, but knowing it doesn't help us at all, because it doesn't represent anything meaningful about the numbers received. It might however be interesting to compare this spate of letters with the numbers received after other incidents and events. This would mean plotting it as a graph instead.

Answer 14    When you make notes about meetings, interviews, conversations etc., it's useful to do this in two stages:

stage 1: make rough notes at the time;
stage 2: go back over them and sort them out.

Answer 15    The two basic rules for filling in forms are:

■ LOOK before you write;
■ THINK before you WRITE.

## 7 Certificate

Completion of this certificate by an authorized person shows that you have worked through all the parts of this workbook and satisfactorily completed the assessments. The certificate provides a record of what you have done that may be used for exemptions or as evidence of prior learning against other nationally certificated qualifications.

Pergamon Flexible Learning and NEBS Management are always keen to refine and improve their products. One of the key sources of information to help this process are people who have just used the product. If you have any information or views, good or bad, please pass these on.

# NEBS MANAGEMENT DEVELOPMENT

# SUPER SERIES

## THIRD EDITION

# Writing Effectively

......................................................................................................

has satisfactorily completed this workbook

Name of signatory  ..............................................................................

Position  ............................................................................................

Signature  ..........................................................................................

Date  ....................................................................

Official stamp

# SUPER SERIES

## SUPER SERIES 3

0-7506-3362-X    Full Set of Workbooks, User Guide and Support Guide

### A. Managing Activities

| | |
|---|---|
| 0-7506-3295-X | 1. Planning and Controlling Work |
| 0-7506-3296-8 | 2. Understanding Quality |
| 0-7506-3297-6 | 3. Achieving Quality |
| 0-7506-3298-4 | 4. Caring for the Customer |
| 0-7506-3299-2 | 5. Marketing and Selling |
| 0-7506-3300-X | 6. Managing a Safe Environment |
| 0-7506-3301-8 | 7. Managing Lawfully - Health, Safety and Environment |
| 0-7506-37064 | 8. Preventing Accidents |
| 0-7506-3302-6 | 9. Leading Change |
| 0-7506-4091-X | 10. Auditing Quality |

### B. Managing Resources

| | |
|---|---|
| 0-7506-3303-4 | 1. Controlling Physical Resources |
| 0-7506-3304-2 | 2. Improving Efficiency |
| 0-7506-3305-0 | 3. Understanding Finance |
| 0-7506-3306-9 | 4. Working with Budgets |
| 0-7506-3307-7 | 5. Controlling Costs |
| 0-7506-3308-5 | 6. Making a Financial Case |
| 0-7506-4092-8 | 7. Managing Energy Efficiency |

### C. Managing People

| | |
|---|---|
| 0-7506-3309-3 | 1. How Organisations Work |
| 0-7506-3310-7 | 2. Managing with Authority |
| 0-7506-3311-5 | 3. Leading Your Team |
| 0-7506-3312-3 | 4. Delegating Effectively |
| 0-7506-3313-1 | 5. Working in Teams |
| 0-7506-3314-X | 6. Motivating People |
| 0-7506-3315-8 | 7. Securing the Right People |
| 0-7506-3316-6 | 8. Appraising Performance |
| 0-7506-3317-4 | 9. Planning Training and Development |
| 0-75063318-2 | 10. Delivering Training |
| 0-7506-3320-4 | 11. Managing Lawfully - People and Employment |
| 0-7506-3321-2 | 12. Commitment to Equality |
| 0-7506-3322-0 | 13. Becoming More Effective |
| 0-7506-3323-9 | 14. Managing Tough Times |
| 0-7506-3324-7 | 15. Managing Time |

### D. Managing Information

| | |
|---|---|
| 0-7506-3325-5 | 1. Collecting Information |
| 0-7506-3326-3 | 2. Storing and Retrieving Information |
| 0-7506-3327-1 | 3. Information in Management |
| 0-7506-3328-X | 4. Communication in Management |
| 0-7506-3329-8 | 5. Listening and Speaking |
| 0-7506-3330-1 | 6. Communicating in Groups |
| 0-7506-3331-X | 7. Writing Effectively |
| 0-7506-3332-8 | 8. Project and Report Writing |
| 0-7506-3333-6 | 9. Making and Taking Decisions |
| 0-7506-3334-4 | 10. Solving Problems |

### SUPER SERIES 3 USER GUIDE + SUPPORT GUIDE

| | |
|---|---|
| 0-7506-37056 | 1. User Guide |
| 0-7506-37048 | 2. Support Guide |

### SUPER SERIES 3 CASSETTE TITLES

| | |
|---|---|
| 0-7506-3707-2 | 1. Complete Cassette Pack |
| 0-7506-3711-0 | 2. Reaching Decisions |
| 0-7506-3712-9 | 3. Making a Financial Case |
| 0-7506-3710-2 | 4. Customers Count |
| 0-7506-3709-9 | 5. Being the Best |
| 0-7506-3708-0 | 6. Working Together |

**To Order** - phone us direct for prices and availability details
(please quote ISBNs when ordering)
College orders: 01865 314333 • Account holders: 01865 314301
Individual purchases: 01865 314627 (please have credit card details ready)

# We Need Your Views

We really need your views in order to make the Super Series 3 (SS3) an even better learning tool for you. Please take time out to complete and return this questionnaire to Management Marketing Department, Pergamon Flexible Learning, Linacre House, Jordan Hill, Oxford, OX2 8DP.

*Name* :....................................................................................................................................

*Address* :................................................................................................................................

.........................................................................................................................................

*Title of workbook* :.................................................................................................................

**If applicable, please state which qualification you are studying for. If not, please describe what study you are undertaking, and with which organisation or college:**

.........................................................................................................................................

**Please grade the following out of 10 (10 being extremely good, 0 being extremely poor):**

Content .............       Appropriateness to your position .............

Readability .............       Qualification coverage .............

**What did you particularly like about this workbook?**

.........................................................................................................................................
.........................................................................................................................................
.........................................................................................................................................

**Are there any features you disliked about this workbook? Please identify them.**

.........................................................................................................................................
.........................................................................................................................................
.........................................................................................................................................

**Are there any errors we have missed?** If so, please state page number: ....................

**How are you using the material?** For example, as an open learning course, as a reference resource, as a training resource etc.

.........................................................................................................................................

**How did you hear about Super Series 3?:**

Word of mouth: ☐      Through my tutor/trainer: ☐      Mailshot: ☐

Other (please give details):.......................................................................................................

.........................................................................................................................................

**Many thanks for your help in returning this form.**